Thirteen Days

A MEMOIR OF THE CUBAN MISSILE CRISIS

Thirteen Days

A MEMOIR OF THE CUBAN MISSILE CRISIS

BY *Robert F. Kennedy*

*With an Afterword by
Richard E. Neustadt and
Graham T. Allison*

HARVARD UNIVERSITY

W · W · NORTON & COMPANY

New York · London

W. W. Norton & Company, Inc., 500 Fifth Avenue, New York, N.Y. 10110
W. W. Norton & Company Ltd., 10 Coptic Street, London, WC1A 1PU

Printed in the United States of America
Library of Congress Catalog Card No. 73–141589

8 9 0

ISBN 0-393-09896-6

Contents

Thirteen Days

A MEMOIR OF THE CUBAN MISSILE CRISIS

"Tuesday morning, October 16, 1962 . . ."

ON TUESDAY MORNING, OCTOBER 16, 1962, shortly after 9:00 o'clock, President Kennedy called and asked me to come to the White House. He said only that we were facing great trouble. Shortly afterward, in his office, he told me that a U-2 had just finished a photographic mission and that the Intelligence Community had become convinced that Russia was placing missiles and atomic weapons in Cuba.

That was the beginning of the Cuban missile crisis—a confrontation between the two giant atomic nations, the U.S. and the U.S.S.R., which brought the world to the abyss of nuclear destruction and the end of mankind. From that moment in President Kennedy's office until Sunday morning, October 28, that was my life—and for Americans and Russians, for the whole world, it was their life as well.

At 11:45 that same morning, in the Cabinet Room, a formal presentation was made by the Central Intelligence Agency to a number of high officials of the government. Photographs were shown to us. Experts arrived with their charts and their pointers and told us that if we looked carefully, we could see there was a missile base being constructed in a field near San Cristobal, Cuba. I, for one, had to take their word for it. I examined the pictures carefully, and what I saw appeared to be no more than the clearing of a field for a farm or the basement of a house. I was relieved to hear later that this was the same reaction of virtually everyone at the meeting, including President Kennedy. Even a few days later, when more work had taken place on the site, he remarked that it looked like a football field.

The dominant feeling at the meeting was stunned surprise. No one had expected or anticipated that the Russians would deploy surface-to-surface ballistic missiles in Cuba. I thought back to my meeting with Soviet Ambassador Anatoly Dobrynin in my office some weeks before. He came to tell me that the Russians were prepared to sign an atmospheric-test-ban treaty if we could make certain agreements on underground testing. I told him I would transmit this message and the accompanying documents to President Kennedy.

I told him we were deeply concerned within the Administration about the amount of military equipment being sent to Cuba. That very morning, I had met on this subject with the President and the Secretaries of

State and Defense. There was some evidence that, in addition to the surface-to-air-missile (SAM) sites that were being erected, the Russians, under the guise of a fishing village, were constructing a large naval shipyard and a base for submarines. This was all being watched carefully—through agents within Cuba who were reporting the military buildup in a limited but frequently important way, through the questioning of refugees who were screened and processed as they arrived in Florida, and through U-2 flights.

It was election time. The autumn days of September and October were filled with charges and countercharges. Republicans "viewing with alarm" were claiming the U.S. was not taking the necessary steps to protect our security. Some, such as Senator Homer E. Capehart of Indiana, were suggesting that we take military action against Cuba.

I told Ambassador Dobrynin of President Kennedy's deep concern about what was happening. He told me I should not be concerned, for he was instructed by Soviet Chairman Nikita S. Khrushchev to assure President Kennedy that there would be no ground-to-ground missiles or offensive weapons placed in Cuba. Further, he said, I could assure the President that this military buildup was not of any significance and that

Khrushchev would do nothing to disrupt the relationship of our two countries during this period prior to the election. Chairman Khrushchev, he said, liked President Kennedy and did not wish to embarrass him.

I pointed out that I felt he had a very strange way of showing his admiration; that what the Russians had been doing in Cuba was a matter of the deepest concern to the United States; and that his protestations of friendship meant little alongside the military activities in the Caribbean. I told him we were watching the buildup carefully and that he should know it would be of the gravest consequence if the Soviet Union placed missiles in Cuba. That would never happen, he assured me, and left.

I reported the conversation to President Kennedy, Secretary of State Dean Rusk, and Secretary of Defense Robert McNamara, and relayed my own skepticism, and suggested that it might be advisable to issue a statement making it unequivocally clear that the U.S. would not tolerate the introduction of offensive surface-to-surface missiles, or offensive weapons of any kind, into Cuba.

That same afternoon, September 4, from a draft prepared by Nicholas Katzenbach, the Deputy Attorney General, and myself, the President issued exactly this

kind of warning and pointed out the serious consequences that would result from such a step.

A week later, on September 11, Moscow dis-
claimed publicly any intention of taking such action and
stated that there was no need for nuclear missiles to be
transferred to any country outside the Soviet Union, including Cuba.

During this same period of time, an important
official in the Soviet Embassy, returning from Moscow,
brought me a personal message from Khrushchev to
President Kennedy, stating that he wanted the President to be assured that under no circumstances would
surface-to-surface missiles be sent to Cuba.

Now, as the representatives of the CIA explained
the U-2 photographs that morning, Tuesday, October
16, we realized that it had all been lies, one gigantic
fabric of lies. The Russians were putting missiles in
Cuba, and they had been shipping them there and beginning the construction of the sites at the same time
those various private and public assurances were being
forwarded by Chairman Khrushchev to President Kennedy.

Thus the dominant feeling was one of shocked
incredulity. We had been deceived by Khrushchev, but
we had also fooled ourselves. No official within the gov-

ernment had ever suggested to President Kennedy that the Russian buildup in Cuba would include missiles. On a number of occasions, the President had asked for a specific evaluation on what the Intelligence Community felt to be the implications for the U.S. of that buildup. The Intelligence Community, in its National Estimate of the future course of events, had advised him—on each of the four occasions in 1962 when they furnished him with official reports on Cuba and the Caribbean— that the Russians would not make offensive weapons available to Cuba. The last estimate before our meeting of the 16th of October was dated the 19th of September, and it advised the President that without reservation the United States Intelligence Board, after considerable discussion and examination, had concluded that the Soviet Union would not make Cuba a strategic base. It pointed out that the Soviet Union had not taken this kind of step with any of its satellites in the past and would feel the risk of retaliation from the United States to be too great to take the risk in this case.

We heard later, in a postmortem study, that reports had come from agents within Cuba indicating the presence of missiles in September of 1962. Most of the reports were false; some were the result of confusion by untrained observers between surface-to-air missiles and surface-to-surface missiles. Several reports, however, turned out to be accurate—one from a former employee at the Hilton Hotel in Havana, who believed a missile installation was being constructed near San Cristobal, and another from someone who overheard Premier Fidel Castro's pilot talking in a boastful and intoxicated way one evening about the nuclear missiles that were going to be furnished Cuba by Russia.

But before these reports were given substance, they had to be checked and rechecked. They were not even considered substantial enough to pass on to the President or other high officials within the government. In retrospect, this was perhaps a mistake. But the same postmortem study also stated that there was no action the U.S. could have taken before the time we actually did act, on the grounds that even the films available on October 16 would not have been substantial enough to convince the governments and peoples of the world of the presence of offensive missiles in Cuba. Certainly, unsubstantiated refugee reports would not have been sufficient.

The important fact, of course, is that the missiles were uncovered and the information was made available to the government and the people before the missiles became operative and in time for the U.S. to act.

The same group that met that first morning in the Cabinet Room met almost continuously through the next twelve days and almost daily for some six weeks thereafter. Others in the group, which was later to be called the "Ex Comm" (the Executive Committee of the National Security Council), included Secretary of State Dean Rusk; Secretary of Defense Robert McNamara; Director of the Central Intelligence Agency John Mc-Cone; Secretary of the Treasury Douglas Dillon; President Kennedy's adviser on national-security affairs, Mc-George Bundy; Presidential Counsel Ted Sorensen; Under Secretary of State George Ball; Deputy Under Secretary of State U. Alexis Johnson; General Maxwell Taylor, Chairman of the Joint Chiefs of Staff; Edward Martin, Assistant Secretary of State for Latin America; originally, Chip Bohlen, who, after the first day, left to become Ambassador to France and was succeeded by Llewellyn Thompson as the adviser on Russian affairs; Roswell Gilpatric, Deputy Secretary of Defense; Paul Nitze, Assistant Secretary of Defense; and, intermittently at various meetings, Vice-President Lyndon B. Johnson; Adlai Stevenson, Ambassador to the United Nations; Ken O'Donnell, Special Assistant to the President; and Don Wilson, who was Deputy Director of the United States Information Agency. This was the group that met, talked, argued, and fought together during that crucial period of time. From this group came the recommendations from which President Kennedy was ultimately to select his course of action.

They were men of the highest intelligence, industrious, courageous, and dedicated to their country's well-being. It is no reflection on them that none was consistent in his opinion from the very beginning to the very end. That kind of open, unfettered mind was essential. For some there were only small changes, perhaps varieties of a single idea. For others there were continuous changes of opinion each day; some, because of the pressure of events, even appeared to lose their judgment and stability.

The general feeling in the beginning was that some form of action was required. There were those, although they were a small minority, who felt the missiles did not alter the balance of power and therefore necessitated no action. Most felt, at that stage, that an air strike against the missile sites could be the only course. Listening to the proposals, I passed a note to the President: "I now know how Tojo felt when he was planning Pearl Harbor."

"The President . . . knew he would have to act."

*A*FTER THE MEETING in the Cabinet Room, I walked back to the Mansion with the President. It would be difficult; the stakes were high—of the highest and most substantial kind—but he knew he would have to act. The U.S. could not accept what the Russians had done. What that action would be was still to be determined. But he was convinced from the beginning that he would have to do something. To keep the discussions from being inhibited and because he did not want to arouse attention, he decided not to attend all the meetings of our committee. This was wise. Personalities change when the President is present, and frequently even strong men make recommendations on the basis of what they believe the President wishes to hear. He instructed our group to come forward with recommendations for one course or possibly several alternative courses of action.

It was during the afternoon and evening of that

first day, Tuesday, that we began to discuss the idea of a quarantine or blockade. Secretary McNamara, by Wednesday, became the blockade's strongest advocate. He argued that it was limited pressure, which could be increased as the circumstances warranted. Further, it was dramatic and forceful pressure, which would be understood yet, most importantly, still leave us in control of events. Later he reinforced his position by reporting that a surprise air strike against the missile bases alone —a surgical air strike, as it came to be called—was militarily impractical in the view of the Joint Chiefs of Staff, that any such military action would have to include all military installations in Cuba, eventually leading to an invasion. Perhaps we would come to that, he argued. Perhaps that course of action would turn out to be inevitable. "But let's not start with that course," if by chance that kind of confrontation with Cuba, and of necessity with the Soviet Union, could be avoided.

Those who argued for the military strike instead of a blockade pointed out that a blockade would not in fact remove the missiles and would not even stop the work from going ahead on the missile sites themselves. The missiles were already in Cuba, and all we would be doing with a blockade would be "closing the door after the horse had left the barn." Further, they argued, we would be bringing about a confrontation with the Soviet Union by stopping their ships, when we should be concentrating on Cuba and Castro.

Their most forceful argument was that our installation of a blockade around Cuba invited the Russians to do the same to Berlin. If we demanded the removal of missiles from Cuba as the price for lifting our blockade, they would demand the removal of missiles surrounding the Soviet Union as the reciprocal act.

And so we argued, and so we disagreed—all dedicated, intelligent men, disagreeing and fighting about the future of their country, and of mankind. Meanwhile, time was slowly running out.

An examination of photography taken on Wednesday, the 17th of October, showed several other installations, with at least sixteen and possibly thirty-two missiles of over a thousand-mile range. Our military experts advised that these missiles could be in operation within a week. The next day, Thursday, estimates by our Intelligence Community placed in Cuba missiles with an atomic-warhead potential of about one half the current ICBM capacity of the entire Soviet Union. The photography having indicated that the missiles were being directed at certain American cities, the estimate was that within a few minutes of their being fired eighty million Americans would be dead.

The members of the Joint Chiefs of Staff were unanimous in calling for immediate military action. They forcefully presented their view that the blockade would not be effective. General Curtis LeMay, Air Force Chief of Staff, argued strongly with the President that a military attack was essential. When the President questioned what the response of the Russians might be, General LeMay assured him there would be no reaction. President Kennedy was skeptical. "They, no more than we, can let these things go by without doing something. They can't, after all their statements, permit us to take out their missiles, kill a lot of Russians, and then do nothing. If they don't take action in Cuba, they certainly will in Berlin."

The President went on to say that he recognized the validity of the arguments made by the Joint Chiefs, the danger that more and more missiles would be placed in Cuba, and the likelihood, if we did nothing, that the Russians would move on Berlin and in other areas of the world, feeling the U.S. was completely impotent. Then it would be too late to do anything in Cuba, for by that time all their missiles would be operational.

General David M. Shoup, Commandant of the Marine Corps, summed up everyone's feelings: "You are in a pretty bad fix, Mr. President." The President answered quickly, "You are in it with me." Everyone laughed, and, with no final decision, the meeting adjourned.

Later, Secretary McNamara, although he told the President he disagreed with the Joint Chiefs and favored a blockade rather than an attack, informed him that the necessary planes, men, and ammunition were being deployed and that we could be ready to move with the necessary air bombardments on Tuesday, October 23, if that was to be the decision. The plans called for an initial attack, consisting of five hundred sorties, striking all military targets, including the missile sites, airfields, ports, and gun emplacements.

I supported McNamara's position in favor of a blockade. This was not from a deep conviction that it would be a successful course of action, but a feeling that it had more flexibility and fewer liabilities than a military attack. Most importantly, like others, I could not accept the idea that the United States would rain bombs on Cuba, killing thousands and thousands of civilians in a surprise attack. Maybe the alternatives were not very palatable, but I simply did not see how we could accept that course of action for our country.

Former Secretary of State Dean Acheson began

attending our meetings, and he was strongly in favor of an air attack. I was a great admirer of his. In 1961, President Kennedy asked him to prepare a report for the National Security Council recommending a course of action to deal with the Russian threat to Berlin. Listening to his presentation then, I had thought to myself that I had never heard anyone so lucid and convincing and would never wish to be on the other side of an argument with him. Now he made his arguments that an air attack and invasion represented our only alternative in the same clear and brilliant way. He said that the President of the United States had the responsibility for the security of the people of the United States and of the whole free world, that it was his obligation to take the only action which could protect that security, and that that meant destroying the missiles.

With some trepidation, I argued that, whatever validity the military and political arguments were for an attack in preference to a blockade, America's traditions and history would not permit such a course of action. Whatever military reasons he and others could marshal, they were nevertheless, in the last analysis, advocating a surprise attack by a very large nation against a very small one. This, I said, could not be undertaken by the U.S. if we were to maintain our moral position at home and around the globe. Our struggle against Communism throughout the world was far more than physical survival—it had as its essence our heritage and our ideals, and these we must not destroy.

We spent more time on this moral question during the first five days than on any other single matter. At various times, it was proposed that we send a letter to Khrushchev twenty-four hours before the bombardment was to begin, that we send a letter to Castro, that leaflets and pamphlets listing the targets be dropped over Cuba before the attack—all these ideas and more were abandoned for military or other reasons. We struggled and fought with one another and with our consciences, for it was a question that deeply troubled us all.

In the midst of all these discussions, Andrei Gromyko came to see the President. It was an appointment made long before the missiles were uncovered, and the President felt it would be awkward to cancel it. He debated whether he should confront the Soviet Foreign Minister with our knowledge of the missiles' presence and finally decided that, as he had not yet determined a final course of action and the disclosure of our knowledge might give the Russians the initiative, he would simply listen to Gromyko.

They met late Wednesday afternoon in the President's office in the White House. Gromyko began the conversation by saying the United States should stop threatening Cuba. All Cuba wanted was peaceful coexistence, he said; she was not interested in exporting her system to other Latin American countries. Cuba, like the Soviet Union, wanted only peace. Premier Khrushchev had instructed him, Gromyko said, to tell President Kennedy that the only assistance being furnished Cuba was for agriculture and land development, so the people could feed themselves, plus a small amount of defensive arms. In view of all the publicity in the American press, he said, he wanted to emphasize that the Soviet Union would never become involved in the furnishing of offensive weapons to Cuba.

Gromyko said he wished to appeal to the U.S. and to President Kennedy on behalf of Premier Khrushchev and the Soviet Union to lessen the tensions that existed with regard to Cuba.

President Kennedy listened, astonished, but also with some admiration for the boldness of Gromyko's position. Firmly, but with great restraint considering the provocation, he told Gromyko that it was not the United States which was fomenting discord, but the Soviet Union. The U.S.S.R.'s supplying of arms to Cuba was having a profound effect on the people of the United

States and was a source of great concern to him. Because of the personal assurances he had received from Khrushchev, he had been taking the public position that no action was required against Cuba, and yet the situation was becoming steadily more dangerous.

Gromyko repeated that the sole objective of the U.S.S.R. was to "give bread to Cuba in order to prevent hunger in that country." As far as arms were concerned, the Soviet Union had simply sent some specialists to train Cubans to handle certain kinds of armament, which were only "defensive." He then said he wished to emphasize the word "defensive" and that none of these weapons could ever constitute a threat to the United States.

The President replied that there should be no misunderstanding of the position of the United States—that that position had been made clear to the Soviet Union in meetings between the Attorney General and Ambassador Dobrynin and in his own public statements. To avoid any misunderstanding, he read aloud his statement of September 4, which pointed out the serious consequences that would arise if the Soviet Union placed missiles or offensive weapons within Cuba.

Gromyko assured him this would never be done, that the United States should not be concerned. After touching briefly on some other matters, he said good-by.

I came by shortly after Gromyko left the White House. The President of the United States, it can be said, was displeased with the spokesman of the Soviet Union. . . .

"A majority opinion . . . for a blockade . . ."

*B*y thursday night, there was a majority opinion in our group for a blockade. Our committee went from the State Department to the White House around 9:15 that night. In order to avoid the suspicion that would have ensued from the presence of a long line of limousines, we all went in my car—John McCone, Maxwell Taylor, the driver, and myself all crowded together in the front seat, and six others sitting in back.

We explained our recommendations to the President. At the beginning, the meeting seemed to proceed in an orderly and satisfactory way. However, as people talked, as the President raised probing questions, minds and opinions began to change again, and not only on small points. For some, it was from one extreme to another—supporting an air attack at the beginning of the meeting and, by the time we left the White House, supporting no action at all.

The President, not at all satisfied, sent us back to

our deliberations. Because any other step would arouse suspicion, he returned to his regular schedule and his campaign speaking engagements.

The next morning, at our meeting at the State Department, there were sharp disagreements again. The strain and the hours without sleep were beginning to take their toll. However, even many years later, those human weaknesses—impatience, fits of anger—are understandable. Each one of us was being asked to make a recommendation which would affect the future of all mankind, a recommendation which, if wrong and if accepted, could mean the destruction of the human race. That kind of pressure does strange things to a human being, even to brilliant, self-confident, mature, experienced men. For some it brings out characteristics and strengths that perhaps even they never knew they had, and for others the pressure is too overwhelming.

Our situation was made more difficult by the fact that there was no obvious or simple solution. A dogmatism, a certainty of viewpoint, was simply not possible. For every position there were inherent weaknesses; and those opposed would point them out, often with devastating effects.

Finally, we agreed on a procedure by which we felt we could give some intelligent recommendations to the President. We knew that time was running out and that delay was not possible. We split into groups to write up our respective recommendations, beginning with an outline of the President's speech to the nation and the whole course of action thereafter, trying to anticipate all possible contingencies and setting forth recommendations as to how to react to them.

In the early afternoon, we exchanged papers, each group dissected and criticized the other, and then the papers were returned to the original group to develop further answers. Gradually from all this came the outline of definitive plans. For the group that advocated the blockade, it was an outline of the legal basis for our action, an agenda for a meeting of the Organization of American States, recommendations for the role of the United Nations, the military procedures for stopping ships, and, finally, the circumstances under which military force might be used. For the group that advocated immediate military action, it was an outline of the areas to be attacked, a defense of our position in the United Nations, suggestions as to how to obtain support from Latin American countries, and a proposed communication to Khrushchev to convince him of the inadvisability of moving militarily against us in the Caribbean, Berlin, or elsewhere in the world.

During all these deliberations, we all spoke as equals. There was no rank, and, in fact, we did not even have a chairman. Dean Rusk—who, as Secretary of State, might have assumed that position—had other duties during this period of time and frequently could not attend our meetings. As a result, with the encouragement of McNamara, Bundy, and Ball, the conversations were completely uninhibited and unrestricted. Everyone had an equal opportunity to express himself and to be heard directly. It was a tremendously advantageous procedure that does not frequently occur within the executive branch of the government, where rank is often so important.

"It was now up to one single man."

WE MET ALL DAY Friday and Friday night. Then again early Saturday morning we were back at the State Department. I talked to the President several times on Friday. He was hoping to be able to meet with us early enough to decide on a course of action and then broadcast it to the nation Sunday night. Saturday morning at 10:00 o'clock I called the President at the Blackstone Hotel in Chicago and told him we were ready to meet with him. It was now up to one single man. No committee was going to make this decision. He canceled his trip and returned to Washington.

As he was returning to Washington, our armed forces across the world were put on alert. Telephoning from our meeting in the State Department, Secretary McNamara ordered four tactical air squadrons placed at readiness for an air strike, in case the President decided to accept that recommendation.

The President arrived back at the White House at 1:40 P.M. and went for a swim. I sat on the side of the pool, and we talked. At 2:30 we walked up to the Oval

Room.

The meeting went on until ten minutes after five. Convened as a formal meeting of the National Security Council, it was a larger group of people who met, some of whom had not participated in the deliberations up to that time. Bob McNamara presented the arguments for the blockade; others presented the arguments for the military attack.

The discussion, for the most part, was able and organized, although, like all meetings of this kind, certain statements were made as accepted truisms, which I, at least, thought were of questionable validity. One member of the Joint Chiefs of Staff, for example, argued that we could use nuclear weapons, on the basis that our adversaries would use theirs against us in an attack. I thought, as I listened, of the many times that I had heard the military take positions which, if wrong, had the advantage that no one would be around at the end to know.

The President made his decision that afternoon in favor of the blockade. There was one final meeting the next morning, with General Walter C. Sweeney, Jr., Commander in Chief of the Tactical Air Command, who told the President that even a major surprise air attack could not be certain of destroying all the missile sites and nuclear weapons in Cuba. That ended the small, lingering doubt that might still have remained in his mind. It had worried him that a blockade would not remove the missiles—now it was clear that an attack could not accomplish that task completely, either.

The strongest argument against the all-out military attack, and one no one could answer to his satisfaction, was that a surprise attack would erode if not destroy the moral position of the United States throughout the world.

Adlai Stevenson had come from New York to attend the meeting Saturday afternoon, as he had attended several of the Ex Comm meetings. He had always been dubious about the air strike, but at the Saturday meeting he strongly advocated what he had only tentatively suggested to me a few days before—namely, that we make it clear to the Soviet Union that if it withdrew its missiles from Cuba, we would be willing to withdraw our missiles from Turkey and Italy and give up our naval base at Guantanamo Bay.

There was an extremely strong reaction from some of the participants to his suggestion, and several sharp exchanges followed. The President, although he rejected Stevenson's suggestion, pointed out that he had for a long period held reservations about the value of

Jupiter missiles in Turkey and Italy and some time ago had asked the State Department to conduct negotiations for their removal; but now, he said, was not the appropriate time to suggest this action, and we could not abandon Guantanamo Bay under threat from the Russians.

Stevenson has since been criticized publicly for the position he took at this meeting. I think it should be emphasized that he was presenting a point of view from a different perspective than the others, one which was therefore important for the President to consider. Although I disagreed strongly with his recommendations, I thought he was courageous to make them, and I might add they made as much sense as some others considered during that period of time.

The President's speech was now scheduled for Monday evening. Under the direction of George Ball, Alex Johnson, and Ed Martin, a detailed hour-to-hour program was arranged, to inform our allies, prepare for the meeting of the OAS, inform the ambassadors stationed in Washington, and prepare for them and others, in written form, the legal justification on which our action was predicated. More and more government officials were brought into the discussions, and finally word began to seep through to the press that a serious crisis was imminent. Through the personal intervention of the President with several newspapers, the only stories written Monday morning were reports that a major speech was to be given by the President and that the country faced a serious crisis.

The diplomatic effort was of great significance. We were able to establish a firm legal foundation for our action under the OAS Charter, and our position around the world was greatly strengthened when the Organization of American States unanimously supported the recommendation for a quarantine. Thus the Soviet Union and Cuba faced the united action of the whole Western Hemisphere. Further, with the support of detailed photographs, Dean Acheson—who obliged the President by once again being willing to help—was able to quickly convince French President Charles de Gaulle of the correctness of our response and later to reassure Chancellor Adenauer. Macmillan made it clear the U.S. would have his country's support. And in these present days of strain, it is well to remember that no country's leader supported the U.S. more forcefully than did France. General de Gaulle said, "It is exactly what I would have done," adding that it was not necessary to see the photographs, as "a great government such as yours does not act without evidence." Chancellor Konrad Adenauer of West Germany voiced his support as well, and the Soviet Union was prevented from separating the U.S. from Europe. (John Diefenbaker, Prime Minister of Canada, was greatly concerned with how to convince the rest of the world.)

All this was done simultaneously with the President's speech and made possible only by the immense work and painstaking planning which preceded it. During this same period, military preparations went forward. Missile crews were placed on maximum alert. Troops were moved into Florida and the southeastern part of the United States. Late Saturday night, the First Armored Division began to move out of Texas into Georgia, and five more divisions were placed on alert. The base at Guantanamo Bay was strengthened.

The Navy deployed one hundred eighty ships into the Caribbean. The Strategic Air Command was dispersed to civilian landing fields around the country, to lessen its vulnerability in case of attack. The B-52 bomber force was ordered into the air fully loaded with atomic weapons. As one came down to land, another immediately took its place in the air.

An hour before the President's speech, Secretary Rusk called in Ambassador Dobrynin and told him of the speech. The newspapers reported that Dobrynin left the Secretary's office looking considerably shaken.

On that Monday afternoon, before his speech and after lunch with Jackie, the President held several meetings. At the first, he formally constituted our committee—which up until that time had been called "the group" or "war council"—under National Security Council Action Memorandum Number 196 as the Executive Committee of the National Security Council, "for the purpose of effective conduct of the operations of the executive branch in the current crisis." The President became the official chairman, and until further notice we were to meet with him every morning at 10:00 A.M.

Shortly thereafter, the President met with the members of the Cabinet and informed them for the first time of the crisis. Then, not long before the broadcast, he met with the leaders of Congress. This was the most difficult meeting. I did not attend, but I know from seeing him afterward that it was a tremendous strain.

Many Congressional leaders were sharp in their criticism. They felt that the President should take more forceful action, a military attack or invasion, and that the blockade was far too weak a response. Senator Richard B. Russell of Georgia said he could not live with himself if he did not say in the strongest possible terms how important it was that we act with greater strength than the President was contemplating.

Senator J. William Fulbright of Arkansas also strongly advised military action rather than such a weak step as the blockade. Others said they were skeptical but would remain publicly silent, only because it was such a dangerous hour for the country.

The President, after listening to the frequently emotional criticism, explained that he would take whatever steps were necessary to protect the security of the United States, but that he did not feel greater military action was warranted initially. Because it was possible that the matter could be resolved without a devastating war, he had decided on the course he had outlined. Perhaps in the end, he said, direct military action would be necessary, but that course should not be followed lightly. In the meantime, he assured them, he had taken measures to prepare our military forces and place them in a position to move.

He reminded them that once an attack began our adversaries could respond with a missile barrage from which many millions of Americans would be killed. That was a gamble he was not willing to take until he had finally and forcefully exhausted all other possibilities. He told them this was an extremely hazardous undertaking and that everyone should understand the

"It was now up to one single man."

risks involved.

He was upset by the time the meeting ended. When we discussed it later he was more philosophical, pointing out that the Congressional leaders' reaction to what we should do, although more militant than his, was much the same as our first reaction when we first heard about the missiles the previous Tuesday.

At 7:00 o'clock, he went on television to the nation to explain the situation in Cuba and the reasons for the quarantine. He was calm and confident that he had selected the right course.

In his speech, he emphasized that the blockade was the *initial* step. He had ordered the Pentagon to make all the preparations necessary for further military action. Secretary McNamara, in a confidential report, had listed the requirements: 250,000 men, 2,000 air sorties against the various targets in Cuba, and 90,000 Marines and Airborne in the invasion force. One estimate of American casualties put the expected figure over 25,000. The President gave his approval for these preparations, and the plans moved ahead. Troops were rapidly moving into the southeastern part of the U.S., equipped and prepared. Arrangements were begun to gather the over a hundred vessels that would be needed for an invasion.

We went to bed that night filled with concern

and trepidation, but filled also with a sense of pride in the strength, the purposefulness, and the courage of the President of the United States. No one could predict what was in store in the days ahead, but we all felt that the President, because of his own wisdom and personal dignity, would have the support of a unified country.

"The important meeting of the OAS..."

*T*HE NEXT DAY, Tuesday, was the important meeting of the OAS previously mentioned. It was anticipated that we might have difficulty obtaining the two thirds vote of support necessary for the ordering of a quarantine. But the Latin American countries, demonstrating a unique sense of unity, unanimously supported the recommendations of the United States. In fact, a number contributed men, supplies, and ships during the several weeks that followed.

Our group met with the President at 10:00 in the morning at the White House. There was a certain spirit of lightness—not gaiety certainly, but a feeling of relaxation, perhaps. We had taken the first step, it wasn't so bad, and we were still alive.

There was much to report. John McCloy, formerly High Commissioner to Germany and an adviser to President Kennedy on European and security matters, had been located in Germany and asked to return and join with Adlai Stevenson in presenting our case to the United Nations. As a Republican, he made our efforts there bipartisan, and as a counterbalance to Stevenson's point of view, he had initially favored a military attack and invasion of Cuba.

John McCone reported to our committee that as yet there had been no general alert of the Soviet forces in Cuba or around the globe. No extraordinary military action of any kind had been reported. In Cuba, the Russians were not permitting anyone other than Russian technical and military personnel to enter the missile bases. He also reported that they were beginning to camouflage the missile sites. It was never clear why they waited until that late date to do so.

The President ordered preparations to proceed for a possible blockade of Berlin. We also discussed in detail what would be done if a U-2 plane were to be shot down, agreeing that—after obtaining specific permission from the President—bomber and fighter planes would destroy a surface-to-air-missile site. Secretary Mc-Namara said that such an attack could take place within two hours after notification of the firing on one of our planes.

By this time, the relaxed, lighter mood had completely disappeared. It had taken only a few minutes.

President Kennedy expressed his deep concern that no error should occur, and that any attack against one of our planes be verified before we return the attack. He asked about the fate of pilots who might be shot down. He then asked Secretary McNamara to put into effect a rescue mission to supplement our U-2 flights. He agreed with Secretary McNamara on extending certain military-personnel tours of duty and on placing the 101st Airborne in readiness for early action. He wanted to make certain that we would have taken all the necessary steps, in case of a military reaction by the Soviets.

"Now, the only thing I say once again is that if the Russians' response makes a military action or invasion inevitable, I want to be able to feel that we will not have to waste any days having to get ready," he said.

At the end of the meeting, the President pointed out that an attack on one of their installations might very well bring an attack against our airfields. He asked for a report from the military as to whether our own planes had been dispersed. When it was reported to him that our photography showed that the Russians and Cubans had inexplicably lined up their planes wing tip to wing tip on Cuban airfields, making them perfect targets, he requested General Taylor to have a U-2 fly a photographic mission over our fields in Florida. "It would be interesting if we have done the same thing," he remarked. We had. He examined the pictures the next day and ordered the Air Force to disperse our planes.

Finally, he made arrangements for regular meetings with ambassadors from the European countries, to prepare for a blockade of Berlin, as well as other contingencies elsewhere. Nothing, whether a weighty matter or small detail, was overlooked.

We came back about 6:00 o'clock that evening. The OAS had announced its support, and the President prepared the proclamation which would put the quarantine into effect at 10:00 o'clock the next morning.

During the course of this meeting, we learned that an extraordinary number of coded messages had been sent to all the Russian ships on their way to Cuba. What they said we did not know then, nor do we know now, but it was clear that the ships as of that moment were still straight on course.

The President composed a letter to Khrushchev, asking him to observe the quarantine legally established by a vote of the OAS, making it clear that the U.S. did not wish to fire on any ships of the Soviet Union, and adding at the end: "I am concerned that we both show prudence and do nothing to allow events to make the situation more difficult to control than it is."

We then discussed in detail the rules that were to be given to the Navy intercepting a merchant vessel in the quarantine zone. To avoid a major military confrontation if a vessel refused to stop, the Navy was to shoot at its rudders and propellers, disabling the vessel but, hopefully, avoiding any loss of life or the sinking of the ship. The President then expressed concern about the boarding of these vessels if the Russians decided to resist. We could anticipate a rough, fierce fight and many casualties, he said. Secretary McNamara felt the vessel might not have to be boarded but would, within a reasonably short period of time, have to be towed into Jacksonville or Charleston.

"What would you do then," the President said, "if we go through all of this effort and then find out there's baby food on it?" Everyone agreed that we should try to intercept the vessels on which there was quite clearly military equipment, but the treatment of other vessels in the meantime posed a serious problem. What criteria could we use for letting some merchant ships through and stopping others? And then how could we be sure?

Our problems for that day were hardly over. John McCone reported that Russian submarines were beginning to move into the Caribbean. One had refueled the day before in the Azores and was headed now toward Cuba. The President ordered the Navy to give the highest priority to tracking the submarines and to put into effect the greatest possible safety measures to protect our own aircraft carriers and other vessels.

After the meeting, the President, Ted Sorensen, Kenny O'Donnell, and I sat in his office and talked. "The great danger and risk in all of this," he said, "is a miscalculation—a mistake in judgment." A short time before, he had read Barbara Tuchman's book *The Guns of August,* and he talked about the miscalculations of the Germans, the Russians, the Austrians, the French, and the British. They somehow seemed to tumble into war, he said, through stupidity, individual idiosyncrasies, misunderstandings, and personal complexes of inferiority and grandeur. We talked about the miscalculation of the Germans in 1939 and the still unfulfilled commitments and guarantees that the British had given to Poland.

Neither side wanted war over Cuba, we agreed, but it was possible that either side could take a step that —for reasons of "security" or "pride" or "face"—would require a response by the other side, which, in turn, for the same reasons of security, pride, or face, would bring about a counterresponse and eventually an escalation into armed conflict. That was what he wanted to avoid. He did not want anyone to be able to say that the U.S. had not done all it could to preserve the peace. We were not going to misjudge, or miscalculate, or challenge the other side needlessly, or precipitously push our adversaries into a course of action that was not intended or anticipated.

Afterward, the President and I talked for a little while alone. He suggested I might visit Ambassador Dobrynin and personally relate to him the serious implications of the Russians' duplicity and the crisis they had created through the presence of their missiles within Cuba.

"I met with Dobrynin . . ."

I CALLED Dobrynin and made arrangements to see him at 9:30 that same Tuesday night. I met with him in his office on the third floor of the Russian Embassy. I reviewed with him the circumstances of the past six weeks which had brought about this confrontation. I pointed out to him that when I had met with him in early September, he had told me that the Russians had not placed any long-range missiles in Cuba and had no intentions of doing so in the future.

He interrupted at that moment and said that was exactly what he had told me and that he had given me his word that the Soviet Union would not put missiles in Cuba that could reach the continental United States.

I said that, based on that statement and the subsequent statement by Tass, the Soviet news agency, the President had taken a less belligerent attitude toward the Soviet Union's actions than other political figures in the U.S. and assured the American people that military action was not necessary against Cuba. Now the President knew he had been deceived, and that had devastating implications for the peace of the world.

Dobrynin's only answer was that he told me there were no missiles in Cuba; that this was what Khrushchev had said, and, as far as he knew, there were still no missiles in Cuba. He then asked me why President Kennedy had not told Gromyko the facts when he had seen him the previous Thursday.

I replied by saying there was nothing the President could tell Gromyko that Gromyko didn't already know—and, after all, why didn't Gromyko tell the President? In fact, the President was shocked that Gromyko's statements even at that late date were so misleading. Dobrynin was extremely concerned. As I left, I asked him if the Soviet ships were going to go through to Cuba. He replied that that had been their instructions and he knew of no changes.

I left the Russian Embassy around 10:15 P.M. and went back to the White House. I found the President meeting Ambassador David Ormsby-Gore of Great Britain, an old friend whom he trusted implicitly. I related the conversation to both of them. The President talked about the possibility of arranging an immediate summit with Khrushchev, but finally dismissed the idea, concluding that such a meeting would be useless until Khrushchev first accepted, as a result of our deeds as well as our statements, the U.S. determination in this matter. Before a summit took place, and it should, the President wanted to have some cards in his own hands.

Ambassador Ormsby-Gore expressed concern that the line of interception for the quarantine had been extended 800 miles. This would mean a probable interception within a very few hours after it was put into effect. "Why not give them more time," he said, "to analyze their position?" The 800 miles had been fixed by the Navy to stay outside the range of some of the MIG fighters in Cuba. The President called McNamara and shortened it to five hundred miles.

The next morning, Wednesday, the quarantine went into effect, and the reports during the early hours told of the Russian ships coming steadily on toward Cuba. I talked with the President for a few moments before we went in to our regular meeting. He said, "It looks really mean, doesn't it? But then, really there was no other choice. If they get this mean on this one in our part of the world, what will they do on the next?" "I just don't think there was any choice," I said, "and not only that, if you hadn't acted, you would have been impeached." The President thought for a moment and said, "That's what I think—I would have been impeached."

The choice was to have gone in and taken steps

which were not necessary or to have acted as we did. At least we now had the support of the whole Western Hemisphere and all our allies around the world.

This Wednesday-morning meeting, along with that of the following Saturday, October 27, seemed the most trying, the most difficult, and the most filled with tension. The Russian ships were proceeding, they were nearing the five-hundred-mile barrier, and we either had to intercept them or announce we were withdrawing. I sat across the table from the President. This was the moment we had prepared for, which we hoped would never come. The danger and concern that we all felt hung like a cloud over us all and particularly over the President.

The U-2s and low-flying planes had returned the previous day with their film, and through the evening it was analyzed—by now in such volume that the film alone was more than twenty-five miles long. The results were presented to us at the meeting. The launching pads, the missiles, the concrete boxes, the nuclear storage bunkers, all the components were there, by now clearly defined and obvious. Comparisons with the pictures of a few days earlier made clear that the work on those sites was proceeding and that within a few days several of the launching pads would be ready for war.

It was now a few minutes after 10:00 o'clock. Secretary McNamara announced that two Russian ships, the *Gagarin* and the *Komiles,* were within a few miles of our quarantine barrier. The interception of both ships would probably be before noon Washington time. Indeed, the expectation was that at least one of the vessels would be stopped and boarded between 10:30 and 11:00 o'clock.

Then came the disturbing Navy report that a Russian submarine had moved into position between the two ships.

It had originally been planned to have a cruiser make the first interception, but, because of the increased danger, it was decided in the past few hours to send in an aircraft carrier supported by helicopters, carrying antisubmarine equipment, hovering overhead. The carrier *Essex* was to signal the submarine by sonar to surface and identify itself. If it refused, said Secretary McNamara, depth charges with a small explosive would be used until the submarine surfaced.

I think these few minutes were the time of gravest concern for the President. Was the world on the brink of a holocaust? Was it our error? A mistake? Was there something further that should have been done? Or not done? His hand went up to his face and covered his mouth. He opened and closed his fist. His face seemed drawn, his eyes pained, almost gray. We stared at each other across the table. For a few fleeting seconds, it was almost as though no one else was there and he was no longer the President.

Inexplicably, I thought of when he was ill and almost died; when he lost his child; when we learned that our oldest brother had been killed; of personal times of strain and hurt. The voices droned on, but I didn't seem to hear anything until I heard the President say: "Isn't there some way we can avoid having our first exchange with a Russian submarine—almost anything but that?" "No, there's too much danger to our ships. There is no alternative," said McNamara. "Our commanders have been instructed to avoid hostilities if at all possible, but this is what we must be prepared for, and this is what we must expect."

We had come to the time of final decision. "We must expect that they will close down Berlin—make the final preparations for that," the President said. I felt we were on the edge of a precipice with no way off. This time, the moment was now—not next week—not tomorrow, "so we can have another meeting and decide"; not in eight hours, "so we can send another message to Khrushchev and perhaps he will finally understand."

No, none of that was possible. One thousand miles away in the vast expanse of the Atlantic Ocean the final decisions were going to be made in the next few minutes. President Kennedy had initiated the course of events, but he no longer had control over them. He would have to wait—we would have to wait. The minutes in the Cabinet Room ticked slowly by. What could we say now —what could we do?

Then it was 10:25—a messenger brought in a note to John McCone. "Mr. President, we have a preliminary report which seems to indicate that some of the Russian ships have stopped dead in the water."

Stopped dead in the water? Which ships? Are they checking the accuracy of the report? Is it true? I looked at the clock. 10:32. "The report is accurate, Mr. President. Six ships previously on their way to Cuba at the edge of the quarantine line have stopped or have turned back toward the Soviet Union. A representative from the Office of Naval Intelligence is on his way over with the full report." A short time later, the report came that the twenty Russian ships closest to the barrier had stopped and were dead in the water or had turned around.

"So no ships will be stopped or intercepted," said the President. I said we should make sure the Navy knew nothing was to be done, that no ships were to be interfered with. Orders would go out to the Navy immediately. "If the ships have orders to turn around, we want to give them every opportunity to do so. Get in direct touch with the *Essex*, and tell them not to do anything, but give the Russian vessels an opportunity to turn back. We must move quickly because the time is expiring," said the President.

Then we were back to the details. The meeting droned on. But everyone looked like a different person. For a moment the world had stood still, and now it was going around again.

"The danger was anything but over."

*D*ESPITE WHAT HAD HAPPENED, the danger was anything but over. We learned later in the day that fourteen of the ships had stopped or had turned back to Russia. Most of those continuing were tankers.

The ship that became the matter of greatest concern was a Russian tanker called the *Bucharest*. During the day, it had reached the barrier, identified itself to one of our naval ships, and, because it was a tanker, been allowed to pass. There was little likelihood that the *Bucharest* carried any missiles or any of the kinds of armament covered by the quarantine. Nevertheless, there were those in the Executive Committee who felt strongly that the *Bucharest* should be stopped and boarded, so that Khrushchev would make no mistake of our will or intent. The President himself emphasized that eventually we would have to stop and board one of the ships approaching Cuba. Those who favored letting the *Bucharest* pass argued that it probably carried no contraband and that Khrushchev needed more time to consider what he should do.

The President postponed a decision and ordered the *Bucharest* shadowed by American warships. At that time, it was proceeding toward Cuba at 17 knots, and a decision had to be made before nightfall.

Meanwhile, the whole world was becoming more and more alarmed. All kinds of people were, officially and unofficially, giving their advice and opinions. Bertrand Russell sent a message to Khrushchev praising him for his conciliatory position and a message to President Kennedy castigating the United States for its warlike attitude. The President took time out of his other deliberations personally to compose an answer: "I think your attention might well be directed to the burglar rather than to those who caught the burglar."

U Thant, Acting Secretary General of the United Nations, suggested that the quarantine be lifted for several weeks if in return the Russians agreed not to send missiles to Cuba. Khrushchev agreed and suggested a summit meeting. President Kennedy responded that the crisis was "created by the secret introduction of offensive weapons into Cuba and the answer lies in the removal of such weapons." He added that we would be happy to have any discussions leading to a satisfactory and peaceful solution, but the missiles in Cuba had to be removed.

"The danger was anything but over."

Adlai Stevenson, at a meeting of the United Nations Security Council, publicly confronted Ambassador V. A. Zorin of the Soviet Union. President Kennedy had made arrangements for photographs of the missile sites to be furnished to Stevenson. Many newspapers around the world, and particularly in Great Britain, were openly skeptical of the U.S. position. At the urgings of Pierre Salinger, the President's Press Secretary, and of Don Wilson, representing the USIA, the President, on October 23, had released the pictures for use at the UN and for publication. Stevenson used them most skillfully in his dramatic televised confrontation with the Russians:

STEVENSON: "Well, let me say something to you, Mr. Ambassador, we do have the evidence. We have it, and it is clear and incontrovertible. And let me say something else. Those weapons must be taken out of Cuba. . . . You, the Soviet Union, have sent these weapons to Cuba. You, the Soviet Union, have created this new danger—not the United States. . . .

"Finally, Mr. Zorin, I remind you that the other day you did not deny the existence of these weapons. But today, again, if I heard you correctly, you now say that they do not exist, or that we haven't proved they exist.

"All right, sir, let me ask you one simple question. Do you, Ambassador Zorin, deny that the U.S.S.R. has placed and is placing medium- and intermediate-range missiles and sites in Cuba? Yes or no? Don't wait for the translation, yes or no?"

ZORIN: "I am not in an American courtroom, sir, and therefore I do not wish to answer a question that is put to me in the fashion in which a prosecutor puts questions. In due course, sir, you will have your answer."

STEVENSON: "You are in the courtroom of world opinion right now, and you can answer yes or no. You have denied that they exist, and I want to know whether I have understood you correctly."

ZORIN: "Continue with your statement. You will have your answer in due course."

STEVENSON: "I am prepared to wait for my answer until hell freezes over, if that's your decision. And I am also prepared to present the evidence in this room."

And with that Stevenson revealed the photographs of the Russian missiles and sites, with devastating effect.

That evening, the President, after further heated discussion, made the final decision permitting the *Bucharest* to go through to Cuba. Against the advice of many of his advisers and of the military, he decided to give Khrushchev more time. "We don't want to push him to a precipitous action—give him time to consider. I don't want to put him in a corner from which he cannot escape."

In the meantime, however, he increased the pressure in other ways. Low-flying flights of eight planes apiece flew over Cuba morning and afternoon, supplementing the photography of the U-2s. All six Russian submarines then in the area or moving toward Cuba from the Atlantic were followed and harassed and, at one time or another, forced to surface in the presence of U.S. military ships.

By now, in the Caribbean surrounding Cuba, we had twenty-five destroyers, two cruisers, several submarines, several carriers, and a large number of support ships.

On the night of Thursday, October 25, our aerial photography revealed that work on the missile sites was proceeding at an extraordinarily rapid pace. By the following evening, October 26, it was clear that the IL-28 bombers were also being rapidly uncrated and assembled.

By this time, an East German passenger ship, carrying some fifteen hundred people, had reached the barrier. Another decision had to be made. Again, there were strong arguments within our group as to what should be done. Again, there were those who urged that the ship be stopped; that it would not directly involve the prestige of the Russians, as it was not a ship of Soviet registry and stopping it would not violate U Thant's request that we not interfere with Russian vessels. The President ultimately decided that the risk of life was so great—with so many people aboard the ship, and so high a possibility of something going seriously wrong—that he would let the vessel through.

"There were almost daily communications with Khrushchev."

*T*HERE WERE almost daily communications with Khrushchev. On Monday, October 22, the day of his speech to the nation, President Kennedy sent a long letter and a copy of his statement directly to the Soviet Chairman. In the course of the letter he said:

"In our discussions and exchanges on Berlin and other international questions, the one thing that has most concerned me has been the possibility that your Government would not correctly understand the will and determination of the United States in any given situation, since I have not assumed that you or any other sane man would, in this nuclear age, deliberately plunge the world into war which it is crystal clear no country could win and which could only result in catastrophic consequences to the whole world, including the aggressor."

Khrushchev, in a letter received October 23, had accused the President of threatening him and the Soviet

Union with the blockade and asserted that it was not going to be observed by the Soviet Union. "The actions of the USA with regard to Cuba are outright banditry or, if you like, the folly of degenerate imperialism." The U.S., he said, was pushing mankind "to the abyss of a world missile-nuclear war," and the Soviet Union would not give instructions to the captains of Soviet vessels bound for Cuba to obey the orders of American naval forces. If any effort to interfere with Soviet ships were to be made, "we would then be forced for our part to take the measures which we deem necessary and adequate in order to protect our rights. For this we have all that is necessary."

The President replied on Thursday, October 25, restating again what had occurred and stressing that— despite private and public assurances that missiles would not be placed in Cuba—that very step had been taken by the Soviet Union.

"In early September I indicated very plainly that the United States would regard any shipment of offensive weapons as presenting the gravest issues. After that time, this Government received the most explicit assurances from your Government and its representatives, both publicly and privately, that no offensive weapons were being sent to Cuba. If you will review the statement issued by Tass in September, you will see how clearly this assurance was given.

"In reliance on these solemn assurances I urged restraint upon those in this country who were urging action in this matter at that time. And then I learned beyond doubt what you have not denied—namely, that all these public assurances were false and that your military people had set out recently to establish a set of missile bases in Cuba. I ask you to recognize clearly, Mr. Chairman, that it was not I who issued the first challenge in this case, and that in the light of this record these activities in Cuba required the responses I have announced.

"I repeat my regret that these events should cause a deterioration in our relations."

And then he added, very simply: "I hope that your Government will take the necessary action to permit a restoration of the earlier situation."

All our efforts and letters, however, seemed to be having little effect. On the contrary, as we waited for the reply to President Kennedy's latest communication with Khrushchev, reports came in that a greater number of Russian personnel were working to expedite the construction of the missile sites and to assemble the IL-28s.

At 7:00 o'clock Friday morning, October 26, the

first vessel was stopped and boarded. She was surely an international ship. It was the *Marucla,* an American-built Liberty ship, Panamanian-owned, registered from Lebanon, and bound for Cuba under a Soviet charter from the Baltic port of Riga. The *Marucla* had been sighted the night before and followed by two destroyers: the *John Pierce* and—a surprise to President Kennedy—the *Joseph P. Kennedy, Jr.,* the destroyer named after the oldest member of our family, who was a Navy pilot and was killed in the Second World War. The *Marucla* had been carefully and personally selected by President Kennedy to be the first ship stopped and boarded. He was demonstrating to Khrushchev that we were going to enforce the quarantine and yet, because it was not a Soviet-owned vessel, it did not represent a direct affront to the Soviets, requiring a response from them. It gave them more time, but simultaneously demonstrated that the U.S. meant business.

At 7:24 A.M., an armed boarding party from both destroyers went alongside the *Marucla* and by 8:00 was aboard and had started the inspection. There were no incidents. The vessel was found to contain no weapons and was allowed to sail on.

The fact that this inspection had been successfully accomplished, however, did not lift the feeling of gloom that was settling over our committee and its deliberations. The Soviet Union had been adamant in its refusal to recognize the quarantine. At the same time, it was obviously preparing its missiles in Cuba for possible use. The President in response ordered a gradual increase in pressure, still attempting to avoid the alternative of direct military action. He increased the number of low-level flights over Cuba from twice a day to once every two hours. Preparations went ahead for night flights, which would take pictures of the missile sites with bright flares that would be dropped across the island. The State Department and the Defense Department were asked to prepare to add petroleum oil and lubricants to the embargo list.

But privately the President was not sanguine about the results of even these efforts. Each hour the situation grew steadily more serious. The feeling grew that this cup was not going to pass and that a direct military confrontation between the two great nuclear powers was inevitable. Both "hawks" and "doves" sensed that our combination of limited force and diplomatic efforts had been unsuccessful. If the Russians continued to be adamant and continued to build up their missile strength, military force would be the only alternative.

"Expect very heavy casualties in an invasion."

*F*RIDAY MORNING President Kennedy ordered the State Department to proceed with preparations for a crash program on civil government in Cuba to be established after the invasion and occupation of that country. Secretary McNamara reported the conclusion of the military that we should expect very heavy casualties in an invasion.

The President turned to us all: "We are going to have to face the fact that, if we do invade, by the time we get to these sites, after a very bloody fight, they will be pointed at us. And we must further accept the possibility that when military hostilities first begin, those missiles will be fired."

John McCone said everyone should understand that an invasion was going to be a much more serious undertaking than most people had previously realized. "They have a hell of a lot of equipment," he said. "And it will be damn tough to shoot them out of those hills, as we learned so clearly in Korea."

Despite the heavy pressure on the big decisions, President Kennedy followed every detail. He requested, for instance, the names of all the Cuban doctors in the Miami area, should their services be required in Cuba. Learning that a U.S. military ship with extremely sensitive equipment (similar to the *Liberty*, which was struck by Israel during the Israeli-Arab war) was very close to the coast of Cuba, he ordered it farther out to sea, where it would be less vulnerable to attack. He supervised everything, from the contents of leaflets to be dropped over Cuba to the assembling of ships for the invasion.

In the meantime, we awaited Khrushchev's answer.

At 6:oo o'clock that night the message came.

A great deal has been written about this message, including the allegation that at the time Khrushchev wrote it he must have been so unstable or emotional that he had become incoherent. There was no question that the letter had been written by him personally. It was very long and emotional. But it was not incoherent, and the emotion was directed at the death, destruction, and anarchy that nuclear war would bring to his people and all mankind. That, he said again and again and in many different ways, must be avoided.

We must not succumb to "petty passions" or to "transient things," he wrote, but should realize that "if indeed war should break out, then it would not be in our power to stop it, for such is the logic of war. I have participated in two wars and know that war ends when it has rolled through cities and villages, everywhere sowing death and destruction." The United States, he went on to say, should not be concerned about the missiles in Cuba; they would never be used to attack the United States and were there for defensive purposes only. "You can be calm in this regard, that we are of sound mind and understand perfectly well that if we attack you, you will respond the same way. But you too will receive the same that you hurl against us. And I think that you also understand this. . . . This indicates that we are normal people, that we correctly understand and correctly evaluate the situation. Consequently, how can we permit the incorrect actions which you ascribe to us? Only lunatics or suicides, who themselves want to perish and to destroy the whole world before they die, could do this."

But he went on: "We want something quite different . . . not to destroy your country . . . but despite our ideological differences, to compete peacefully, not by military means."

There was no purpose, he said, for us to interfere with any of his ships now bound for Cuba, for they contained no weapons. He then explained why they carried no missiles: all the shipments of weapons were already within Cuba. This was the first time he had acknowledged the presence of missiles in Cuba. He made reference to the landing at the Bay of Pigs and the fact that President Kennedy had told him in Vienna that this was a mistake. He valued such frankness, wrote Khrushchev, and he, too, had similar courage, for he had acknowledged "those mistakes which had been committed during the history of our state and I not only acknowledge but sharply condemned them." (President Kennedy had told him in Vienna that he was quick to acknowledge and condemn the mistakes of Stalin and others, but he never acknowledged any mistakes of his own.)

The reason he had sent these weapons to Cuba was because the U.S. was interested in overthrowing the Cuban government, as the U.S. had actively attempted to overthrow the Communist government in the Soviet Union after their revolution. Khrushchev and the Soviet people wished to help Cuba protect herself.

But then he went on: "If assurances were given that the President of the United States would not participate in an attack on Cuba and the blockade lifted, then the question of the removal or the destruction of the missile sites in Cuba would then be an entirely different question. Armaments bring only disasters. When one accumulates them, this damages the economy, and if one puts them to use, then they destroy people on both sides. Consequently, only a madman can believe that armaments are the principal means in the life of society. No, they are an enforced loss of human energy, and what is more are for the destruction of man himself. If people do not show wisdom, then in the final analysis they will come to a clash, like blind moles, and then reciprocal extermination will begin."

This is my proposal, he said. No more weapons to Cuba and those within Cuba withdrawn or destroyed, and you reciprocate by withdrawing your blockade and also agree not to invade Cuba. Don't interfere, he said, in a piratical way with Russian ships. "If you have not lost your self-control and sensibly conceive what this might lead to, then, Mr. President, we and you ought not to pull on the ends of the rope in which you have tied the knot of war, because the more the two of us pull, the tighter the knot will be tied. And a moment may come when that knot will be tied so tight that even he who tied it will not have the strength to untie it, and then it will be necessary to cut that knot, and what that would mean is not for me to explain to you, because you your-self understand perfectly of what terrible forces our countries dispose. Consequently, if there is no intention to tighten that knot, and thereby to doom the world to the catastrophe of thermonuclear war, then let us not only relax the forces pulling on the ends of the rope, let us take measures to untie that knot. We are ready for this."

The message was examined and re-examined at a meeting we held late Friday night. As the hours went on into the morning, it was finally decided that the State Department would come forward with an analysis and some recommendations on how it should be answered; that we would meet again early Saturday morning, October 27.

I had a slight feeling of optimism as I drove home from the State Department that night. The letter, with all its rhetoric, had the beginnings perhaps of some ac-commodation, some agreement. The feeling was strengthened by the fact that John Scali, a very able and experienced reporter for ABC, had been approached by an important official of the Soviet Embassy with a pro-posal that the Soviet Union would remove the missiles under United Nations supervision and inspection and the U.S. would lift the blockade and give a pledge not to invade Cuba as its part of the understanding. He was asked to transmit this message to the United States government, which he had immediately done.

Why they selected this means of communication was not clear, but an unorthodox procedure of this kind was not unusual for the Soviet Union.

I was also slightly more optimistic because when I left the President that night, he too was for the first time hopeful that our efforts might possibly be successful.

"This would mean war."

*O*N SATURDAY MORNING, October 27, I received a memorandum from J. Edgar Hoover, Director
of the Federal Bureau of Investigation, that gave me a
feeling of considerable disquiet. He had received information the night before that certain Soviet personnel in
New York were apparently preparing to destroy all sensitive documents on the basis that the U.S. would probably be taking military action against Cuba or Soviet
ships, and this would mean war. I asked myself as I
drove to the White House: If the Soviets were anxious to
find an answer to the crisis, why this conduct on the part
of Soviet personnel? Did the Khrushchev letter really
indicate a solution could be found?

It was therefore with some sense of foreboding
that I went to the meeting of our Ex Comm. My concern
was justified. A new, this time very formal, letter had
arrived from Khrushchev to President Kennedy. It was
obviously no longer Mr. Khrushchev personally who
was writing, but the Foreign Office of the Kremlin. The
letter was quite different from the letter received

twelve hours before. "We will remove our missiles from Cuba, you will remove yours from Turkey. . . . The Soviet Union will pledge not to invade or interfere with the internal affairs of Turkey; the U.S. to make the same pledge regarding Cuba."

To add to the feeling of foreboding and gloom, Secretary McNamara reported increased evidence that the Russians in Cuba were now working day and night, intensifying their efforts on all the missile sites and on the IL-28s. Thus began the most difficult twenty-four hours of the missile crisis.

The fact was that the proposal the Russians made was not unreasonable and did not amount to a loss to the U.S. or to our NATO allies. On several occasions over the period of the past eighteen months, the President had asked the State Department to reach an agreement with Turkey for the withdrawal of Jupiter missiles in that country. They were clearly obsolete, and our Polaris submarines in the Mediterranean would give Turkey far greater protection.

At the President's insistence, Secretary Rusk had raised the question with the representatives of Turkey following a NATO meeting in the spring of 1962. The Turks objected, and the matter was permitted to drop. In the summer of 1962, when Rusk was in Europe, President Kennedy raised the question again. He was told by the State Department that they felt it unwise to press the matter with Turkey. But the President disagreed. He wanted the missiles removed even if it would cause political problems for our government. The State Department representatives discussed it again with the Turks and, finding they still objected, did not pursue the matter.

The President believed he was President and that, his wishes having been made clear, they would be followed and the missiles removed. He therefore dismissed the matter from his mind. Now he learned that the failure to follow up on this matter had permitted the same obsolete Turkish missiles to become hostages of the Soviet Union.

He was angry. He obviously did not wish to order the withdrawal of the missiles from Turkey under threat from the Soviet Union. On the other hand, he did not want to involve the U.S. and mankind in a catastrophic war over missile sites in Turkey that were antiquated and useless. He pointed out to the State Department and the others that, to reasonable people, a trade of this kind might look like a very fair suggestion, that our position had become extremely vulnerable, and that it was our own fault.

The change in the language and tenor of the letters from Khrushchev indicated confusion within the Soviet Union; but there was confusion among us as well. At that moment, not knowing exactly what to suggest, some recommended writing to Khrushchev and asking him to clarify his two letters. There was no clear course of action. Yet we realized that, as we sat there, the work was proceeding on the missile sites in Cuba, and we now had the additional consideration that if we destroyed these sites and began an invasion, the door was clearly open for the Soviet Union to take reciprocal action against Turkey.

The NATO countries were supporting our position and recommending that the U.S. be firm; but, President Kennedy said, they did not realize the full implications for them. If we carried out an air strike against Cuba and the Soviet Union answered by attacking Turkey, all NATO was going to be involved. Then, immediately, the President would have to decide whether he would use nuclear weapons against the Soviet Union, and all mankind would be threatened.

The Joint Chiefs of Staff joined the meeting and recommended their solution. It had the attraction of being a very simple next step—an air strike on Monday, followed shortly afterward by an invasion. They pointed out to the President that they had always felt the block-ade to be far too weak a course and that military steps were the only ones the Soviet Union would understand. They were not at all surprised that nothing had been achieved by limited force, for this is exactly what they had predicted.

In the midst of these deliberations, another mes-sage came, to change the whole course of events and al-ter history. Major Rudolf Anderson, Jr., from South Car-olina, one of the two Air Force pilots who had carried out the original U-2 reconnaissance that uncovered the presence of missiles in Cuba, had since flown several other photo-reconnaissance missions and was flying one that Saturday morning, October 27. Our meeting was in-terrupted by the report that his plane had been hit by a SAM missile, that it had crashed in Cuba, and that he had been killed.

There was sympathy for Major Anderson and his family. There was the knowledge that we had to take military action to protect our pilots. There was the reali-zation that the Soviet Union and Cuba apparently were preparing to do battle. And there was the feeling that the noose was tightening on all of us, on Americans, on mankind, and that the bridges to escape were crum-bling.

"How can we send any more U-2 pilots into this area tomorrow unless we take out all of the SAM sites?" the President asked. "We are now in an entirely new ball game."

At first, there was almost unanimous agreement that we had to attack early the next morning with bombers and fighters and destroy the SAM sites. But again the President pulled everyone back. "It isn't the first step that concerns me," he said, "but both sides escalating to the fourth and fifth step—and we don't go to the sixth because there is no one around to do so. We must remind ourselves we are embarking on a very hazardous course."

He asked for absolute verification that the U-2 was shot down and did not crash accidentally, and for a careful review, "before we decide finally what we shall do," of the implications of all possible courses of action. His mind went to other areas of the world. What was going to occur in Berlin, in Turkey? If we attacked Cuba, and the Russians reciprocated with an attack on Turkey, would or should the Turkish missiles be fired? He ordered preparations taken to defuse missiles with atomic warheads, so that he personally would have to give permission before they were used. What role should Turkey and the rest of NATO have in determining our response? Within a very short time, they might be faced with decisions of life and death. Before that happened, should they not have a right to learn, if not pass on, what we were deciding to do, particularly if that was likely to affect them in such a rapid and possibly devastating way?

Again and again he emphasized that we must understand the implications of every step. What response could we anticipate? What were the implications for us? He stressed again our responsibility to consider the effect our actions would have on others. NATO was supporting the United States, but were these countries truly and completely aware of the dangers for them? These hourly decisions, necessarily made with such rapidity, could be made only by the President of the United States, but any one of them might close and lock doors for peoples and governments in many other lands. We had to be aware of this responsibility at all times, he said, aware that we were deciding, the President was deciding, for the U.S., the Soviet Union, Turkey, NATO, and really for all mankind. . . .

"Those hours in the Cabinet Room . . ."

*T*HOSE HOURS in the Cabinet Room that Saturday afternoon in October could never be erased from the minds of any of us. We saw as never before the meaning and responsibility involved in the power of the United States, the power of the President, the responsibility we had to people around the globe who had never heard of us, who had never heard of our country or the men sitting in that room determining their fate, making a decision which would influence whether they would live or die.

We won't attack tomorrow, the President said. We shall try again.

The State Department submitted a draft of a letter for response from President Kennedy to Khrushchev. It answered the arguments made in Khrushchev's latest letter, maintaining that we could not remove the missiles from Turkey and that no trade could be made.

I disagreed with the content and tenor of the letter. I suggested, and was supported by Ted Sorensen and others, that we ignore the latest Khrushchev letter and respond to his earlier letter's proposal, as refined in the offer made to John Scali, that the Soviet missiles and offensive weapons would be removed from Cuba under UN inspection and verification if, on its side, the United States would agree with the rest of the Western Hemisphere not to invade Cuba.

There were arguments back and forth. There were sharp disagreements. Everyone was tense; some were already near exhaustion; all were weighted down with concern and worry. President Kennedy was by far the calmest. Finally, when we almost seemed unable to communicate with one another, he suggested with a note of some exasperation that—inasmuch as I felt so strongly that the State Department's various efforts to respond were not satisfactory—Ted Sorensen and I should leave the meeting and go into his office and compose an alternative response, so he could then decide between the two. The two of us left and, sitting in the President's office, wrote a draft. Forty-five minutes later, we took it to him and to the whole group. He worked on it, refined it, had it typed, and signed it.

It accepted Khrushchev's "offer":

"Dear Mr. Chairman:

"I have read your letter of October 26th with great care and welcomed the statement of your desire to seek a prompt solution to the problem. The first thing that needs to be done, however, is for work to cease on offensive missile bases in Cuba and for all weapons systems in Cuba capable of offensive use to be rendered inoperable, under effective United Nations arrangements.

"Assuming this is done promptly, I have given my representatives in New York instructions that will permit them to work out this weekend—in cooperation with the Acting Secretary General and your representative—an arrangement for a permanent solution to the Cuban problem along the lines suggested in your letter of October 26th. As I read your letter, the key elements of your proposals—which seem generally acceptable as I understand them—are as follows:

"1. You would agree to remove these weapons systems from Cuba under appropriate United Nations observation and supervision; and undertake, with suitable safeguards, to halt the further introduction of such weapons systems into Cuba.

"2. We, on our part, would agree—upon the establishment of adequate arrangements through the United Nations to ensure the carrying out and continuation of these commitments—(a) to remove promptly the quarantine measures now in effect, and (b) to give assurances against an invasion of Cuba. I am confident that other nations of the Western Hemisphere would be prepared to do likewise.

"If you will give your representative similar instructions, there is no reason why we should not be able to complete these arrangements and announce them to the world within a couple of days. The effect of such a settlement on easing world tensions would enable us to work toward a more general arrangement regarding 'other armaments,' as proposed in your second letter, which you made public. I would like to say again that the United States is very much interested in reducing tensions and halting the arms race; and if your letter signifies that you are prepared to discuss a detente affecting NATO and the Warsaw Pact, we are quite prepared to consider with our allies any useful proposals.

· "But the first ingredient, let me emphasize, is the cessation of work on missile sites in Cuba and measures to render such weapons inoperable, under effective international guarantees. The continuation of this threat, or a prolonging of this discussion concerning Cuba by linking these problems to the broader questions of European and world security, would surely lead to an intensification of the Cuban crisis and a grave risk to the peace of the world. For this reason, I hope we can quickly agree along the lines outlined in this letter and in your letter of October 26th.

"John F. Kennedy"

"The President ordered the
Ex Comm . . ."

*T*HE PRESIDENT ordered the Ex Comm to meet again at 9:00 P.M. in the White House. While the letter was being typed and prepared for transmission, he and I sat in his office. He talked about Major Anderson and how it is always the brave and the best who die. The politicians and officials sit home pontificating about great principles and issues, make the decisions, and dine with their wives and families, while the brave and the young die. He talked about the miscalculations that lead to war. War is rarely intentional. The Russians don't wish to fight any more than we do. They do not want to war with us nor we with them. And yet if events continue as they have in the last several days, that struggle—which no one wishes, which will accomplish nothing—will engulf and destroy all mankind.

He wanted to make sure that he had done everything in his power, everything conceivable, to prevent such a catastrophe. Every opportunity was to be given to the Russians to find a peaceful settlement which would not diminish their national security or be a public humiliation. It was not only for Americans that he was concerned, or primarily the older generation of any land. The thought that disturbed him the most, and that made the prospect of war much more fearful than it would otherwise have been, was the specter of the death of the children of this country and all the world—the young people who had no role, who had no say, who knew nothing even of the confrontation, but whose lives would be snuffed out like everyone else's. They would never have a chance to make a decision, to vote in an election, to run for office, to lead a revolution, to determine their own destinies.

Our generation had. But the great tragedy was that, if we erred, we erred not only for ourselves, our futures, our hopes, and our country, but for the lives, futures, hopes, and countries of those who had never been given an opportunity to play a role, to vote aye or nay, to make themselves felt.

It was this that troubled him most, that gave him such pain. And it was then that he and Secretary Rusk decided that I should visit with Ambassador Dobrynin and personally convey the President's great concern.

I telephoned Ambassador Dobrynin about 7:15 P.M. and asked him to come to the Department of Justice. We met in my office at 7:45. I told him first that we knew that work was continuing on the missile bases in Cuba and that in the last few days it had been expedited. I said that in the last few hours we had learned that our reconnaissance planes flying over Cuba had been fired upon and that one of our U-2s had been shot down and the pilot killed. That for us was a most serious turn of events.

President Kennedy did not want a military conflict. He had done everything possible to avoid a military engagement with Cuba and with the Soviet Union, but now they had forced our hand. Because of the deception of the Soviet Union, our photographic reconnaissance planes would have to continue to fly over Cuba, and if the Cubans or Soviets shot at these planes, then we would have to shoot back. This would inevitably lead to further incidents and to escalation of the conflict, the implications of which were very grave indeed.

He said the Cubans resented the fact that we were violating Cuban air space. I replied that if we had not violated Cuban air space, we would still be believing what Khrushchev had said—that there would be no missiles placed in Cuba. In any case, I said, this matter was far more serious than the air space of Cuba—it involved the peoples of both of our countries and, in fact, people all over the globe.

The Soviet Union had secretly established missile bases in Cuba while at the same time proclaiming privately and publicly that this would never be done. We had to have a commitment by tomorrow that those bases would be removed. I was not giving them an ultimatum but a statement of fact. He should understand that if they did not remove those bases, we would remove them. President Kennedy had great respect for the Ambassador's country and the courage of its people. Perhaps his country might feel it necessary to take retaliatory action; but before that was over, there would be not only dead Americans but dead Russians as well.

He asked me what offer the United States was making, and I told him of the letter that President Kennedy had just transmitted to Khrushchev. He raised the question of our removing the missiles from Turkey. I said that there could be no quid pro quo or any arrangement made under this kind of threat or pressure, and that in the last analysis this was a decision that would have to be made by NATO. However, I said, President Kennedy had been anxious to remove those missiles from Turkey and Italy for a long period of time. He had ordered their removal some time ago, and it was our judgment that, within a short time after this crisis was over, those missiles would be gone.

I said President Kennedy wished to have peaceful relations between our two countries. He wished to resolve the problems that confronted us in Europe and Southeast Asia. He wished to move forward on the control of nuclear weapons. However, we could make progress on these matters only when the crisis was behind us. Time was running out. We had only a few more hours— we needed an answer immediately from the Soviet Union. I said we must have it the next day.

I returned to the White House. The President was not optimistic, nor was I. He ordered twenty-four troop-carrier squadrons of the Air Force Reserve to active duty. They would be necessary for an invasion. He had not abandoned hope, but what hope there was now rested with Khrushchev's revising his course within the next few hours. It was a hope, not an expectation. The expectation was a military confrontation by Tuesday and possibly tomorrow. . . .

I had promised my daughters for a long time that I would take them to the Horse Show, and early Sunday morning I went to the Washington Armory to watch the horses jump. In any case, there was nothing I could do but wait. Around 10:00 o'clock, I received a call at the Horse Show. It was Secretary Rusk. He said he had just received word from the Russians that they had agreed to withdraw the missiles from Cuba.

I went immediately to the White House, and there I received a call from Ambassador Dobrynin, saying he would like to visit with me. I met him in my office at 11:00 A.M.

He told me that the message was coming through that Khrushchev had agreed to dismantle and withdraw the missiles under adequate supervision and inspection; that everything was going to work out satisfactorily; and that Mr. Khrushchev wanted to send his best wishes to the President and to me.

It was quite a different meeting from the night before. I went back to the White House and talked to the President for a long time. While I was there, he placed telephone calls to former Presidents Truman and Eisenhower. As I was leaving, he said, making reference to Abraham Lincoln, "This is the night I should go to the theater." I said, "If you go, I want to go with you." As I closed the door, he was seated at the desk writing a letter to Mrs. Anderson. . . .

"Some of the things we learned . . ."

I OFTEN THOUGHT afterward of some of the things we learned from this confrontation. The time that was available to the President and his advisers to work secretly, quietly, privately, developing a course of action and recommendations for the President, was essential. If our deliberations had been publicized, if we had had to make a decision in twenty-four hours, I believe the course that we ultimately would have taken would have been quite different and filled with far greater risks. The fact that we were able to talk, debate, argue, disagree, and then debate some more was essential in choosing our ultimate course. Such time is not always present, although, perhaps surprisingly, on most occasions of great crisis it is; but when it is, it should be utilized.

But more than time is necessary. I believe our deliberations proved conclusively how important it is that the President have the recommendations and opinions of more than one individual, of more than one department, and of more than one point of view. Opinion, even fact itself, can best be judged by conflict, by debate. There is an important element missing when there is unanimity of viewpoint. Yet that not only can happen; it frequently does when the recommendations are being given to the President of the United States. His office creates such respect and awe that it has almost a cowering effect on men. Frequently I saw advisers adapt their opinions to what they believed President Kennedy and, later, President Johnson wished to hear.

I once attended a preliminary meeting with a Cabinet officer, where we agreed on a recommendation to be made to the President. It came as a slight surprise to me when, a few minutes later, in the meeting with the President himself, the Cabinet officer vigorously and fervently expressed the opposite point of view, which, from the discussion, he quite accurately learned would be more sympathetically received by the President.

We had virtual unanimity at the time of the Bay of Pigs. At least, if any officials in the highest ranks of government were opposed, they did not speak out. Thereafter, I suggested there be a devil's advocate to give an opposite opinion if none was pressed. At the time of the Cuban missile crisis, this was obviously not needed.

It is also important that different departments of

government be represented. Thirty years ago, the world was a far, far different place. The Secretary of State and his department could handle all international problems. Perhaps they were not always handled correctly, but at least this handling by one department was manageable. Our commitments were few—we were not as widely involved as we are today—but we were nevertheless a very powerful nation. We could and did, in places we felt our national interests were involved (such as Latin America), impose our will by force if we believed it necessary. The Secretary of State dealt with all the responsibilities without great difficulty, giving foreign-policy advice to the President, administering the department, directing our relationships with that handful of countries which were considered significant, and protecting the financial interests of our citizens around the world.

But that position has very little relationship with that of the Secretary of State today. The title is the same; it still deals with foreign affairs; but there the similarity virtually disappears. Today, the Secretary of State's position is at least five jobs, five different areas of responsibility, all of which could properly require his full time.

The Secretary of State must deal with more than one hundred twenty countries, attend to the affairs of the United Nations, and travel to numerous countries.

He must receive ambassadors, attend dinners, and handle other protocol and social affairs (and lest anyone believe this to be unimportant, we might remember that Secretary Rusk missed President Kennedy's extremely important meeting with Prime Minister Macmillan in Nassau because of a diplomatic dinner he felt he should attend). The Secretary of State must deal with a dozen crises of various significance that arise every week all over the globe, in the Congo, Nigeria, Indonesia, Aden, or elsewhere. He must deal with the one or two major crises that seem to be always with us, such as Berlin in 1961, Cuba in 1962, and now Vietnam. Finally, he must administer one of the largest and most complicated of all departments.

Beyond the time and energy that are required in administering the office, there is another major difference in foreign affairs. Thirty years ago, only the State Department was involved in international matters. But that is no longer true. A number of other agencies and departments have primary responsibilities and power in the foreign-relations field, including the Pentagon, the CIA, the Agency for International Development, and, to a lesser degree, the USIA and other independent or semi-independent departments.

In some countries of the world, the most powerful single voice is that of the AID administrator, with the Ambassador—even though he is representing the State Department and is ostensibly the chief spokesman for the United States and its President—having relatively little power. In some countries that I visited, the dominant U.S. figure was the representative of the CIA; in several of the Latin American countries, it was the head of our military mission. In all these countries, an important role was played by the USIA and, to a lesser degree, the Peace Corps, the Export-Import Bank, the American business community in general, and, in certain countries, particular businessmen.

Individual representatives of at least the Pentagon, the CIA, and AID must be heard and listened to by the President of the United States in addition to the State Department. They have information, intelligence, opinions, and judgments which may be invaluable and which may be quite different from those of the State Department.

It is also true that because of the heavy responsibility of the Secretary of State, he cannot possibly keep himself advised on the details of every crisis with which his department has to deal. There is also the risk that as information is sifted through a number of different hands up to him or to the President, vital facts may be eliminated or distorted through an error of judgment. Thus it is essential for a President to have personal access to those within the department who have expertise and knowledge. He can in this way have available unfiltered information to as great a degree as is practical and possible.

During the Cuban missile crisis, the President not only received information from all the significant departments, but went to considerable lengths to ensure that he was not insulated from individuals or points of view because of rank or position. He wanted the advice of his Cabinet officers, but he also wanted the opinion of those who were connected with the situation itself. He wanted to hear from Secretary Rusk, but he also wished to hear from Tommy Thompson, former (and now again) Ambassador to the Soviet Union, whose advice on the Russians and predictions as to what they would do were uncannily accurate and whose advice and recommendations were surpassed by none; from Ed Martin, Assistant Secretary for Latin America, who organized our effort to secure the backing of the Latin American countries; also from George Ball, the Under Secretary of State, whose advice and judgment were invaluable. He wanted to hear from Secretary McNamara, but he wanted to hear also from Under Secretary Gilpatric, whose ability, knowledge, and judgment he sought in every serious crisis.

On other occasions, I had frequently observed efforts being made to exclude certain individuals from participating in a meeting with the President because they held a different point of view. Often, the President would become aware of this fact and enlarge the meetings to include other opinions. At the missile-crisis conferences he made certain there were experts and representatives of different points of view. President Kennedy wanted people who raised questions, who criticized, on whose judgment he could rely, who presented an intelligent point of view, regardless of their rank or viewpoint.

He wanted to hear presented and challenged all the possible consequences of a particular course of action. The first step might appear sensible, but what would be the reaction of our adversaries and would we actually stand to gain? I remember an earlier meeting on Laos, in 1961, when the military unanimously recommended sending in substantial numbers of U.S. troops to stabilize the country. They were to be brought in through two airports with limited capability. Someone questioned what we would do if only a limited number landed and then the Communist Pathet Lao knocked out the airports and proceeded to attack our troops, limited in number and not completely equipped. The representatives of the military said we would then have to destroy Hanoi and possibly use nuclear weapons. President Kennedy did not send in the troops and concentrated on diplomatic steps to protect our interests.

It was to obtain an unfettered and objective analysis that he frequently, and in critical times, invited Secretary of the Treasury Douglas Dillon, for whose wisdom he had such respect; Kenny O'Donnell, his appointment secretary; Ted Sorensen; and, at times, former Secretary of State Dean Acheson, former Secretary of Defense Robert Lovett, former High Commissioner of Germany John McCloy, and others. They asked the difficult questions; they made others defend their position; they presented a different point of view; and they were skeptical.

I think this was more necessary in the military field than any other. President Kennedy was impressed with the effort and dedicated manner in which the military responded—the Navy deploying its vessels into the Caribbean; the Air Force going on continuous alert; the Army and the Marines moving their soldiers and equipment into the southeastern part of the U.S.; and all of them alert and ready for combat.

But he was distressed that the representatives with whom he met, with the notable exception of General Taylor, seemed to give so little consideration to the implications of steps they suggested. They seemed always to assume that if the Russians and the Cubans would not respond or, if they did, that a war was in our national interest. One of the Joint Chiefs of Staff once said to me he believed in a preventive attack against the Soviet Union. On that fateful Sunday morning when the Russians answered they were withdrawing their missiles, it was suggested by one high military adviser that we attack Monday in any case. Another felt that we had in some way been betrayed.

President Kennedy was disturbed by this inability to look beyond the limited military field. When we talked about this later, he said we had to remember that they were trained to fight and to wage war—that was their life. Perhaps we would feel even more concerned if they were always opposed to using arms or military means—for if they would not be willing, who would be? But this experience pointed out for us all the importance of civilian direction and control and the importance of raising probing questions to military recommendations.

It was for these reasons, and many more, that

President Kennedy regarded Secretary McNamara as the most valuable public servant in his Administration and in the government.

From all this probing and examination—of the military, State Department, and their recommendations—President Kennedy hoped that he would at least be prepared for the foreseeable contingencies and know that—although no course of action is ever completely satisfactory—he had made his decision based on the best possible information. His conduct of the missile crisis showed how important this kind of skeptical probing and questioning could be.

It also showed how important it was to be respected around the world, how vital it was to have allies and friends. Now, five years later, I discern a feeling of isolationism in Congress and through the country, a feeling that we are too involved with other nations, a resentment of the fact that we do not have greater support in Vietnam, an impression that our AID program is useless and our alliances dangerous. I think it would be well to think back to those days in October 1962.

We have not always had the support of Latin American countries in everything we have done. Frequently, our patience has been sorely tried by the opposition of some of the larger South American countries to measures we felt to be in our common interest and worthy of their support. During the Cuban missile crisis, however, when it was an issue of the greatest importance, when the United States was being sorely tried, those countries came unanimously to our support, and that support was essential.

It was the vote of the Organization of American States that gave a legal basis for the quarantine. Their willingness to follow the leadership of the United States was a heavy and unexpected blow to Khrushchev. It had a major psychological and practical effect on the Russians and changed our position from that of an outlaw acting in violation of international law into a country acting in accordance with twenty allies legally protecting their position.

Similarly, the support of our NATO allies—the rapid public acceptance of our position by Adenauer, de Gaulle, and Macmillan—was of great importance. They accepted our recitation of the facts without question and publicly supported our position without reservation. Had our relationship of trust and mutual respect not been present, had our NATO allies been skeptical about what we were doing and its implications for them, and had Khrushchev thus been able to split off the NATO countries or even one of our chief allies, our position would have been seriously undermined.

Even in Africa, support from a number of countries that had been considered antagonistic toward the United States was of great significance. With a naval quarantine around Cuba, our military reported, Soviet planes could still fly atomic warheads into Cuba. To do so they had to refuel in West Africa, and the critical countries with sufficiently large airports and the necessary refueling facilities were Guinea and Senegal. President Kennedy sent our two Ambassadors to see the Presidents of those two countries.

Sekou Touré of Guinea had been the subject of great criticism in the United States because of his friendship with the Communist nations; but he also admired President Kennedy. When our Ambassador visited him, he immediately accepted as true President Kennedy's description of what was happening in Cuba; said Guinea was not going to assist any country in constructing a military base on foreign soil; and announced that Russian planes would not be permitted to refuel in Conakry.

In Dakar, Ambassador Philip M. Kaiser had a close personal relationship with President Leopold Senghor, who a short time before had had a very successful visit to Washington. He, too, quickly perceived the danger and agreed not to permit Russian planes to land or refuel in Dakar.

In short, our friends, our allies, and, as Thomas Jefferson said, a respect for the opinions of mankind, are all vitally important. We cannot be an island even if we wished; nor can we successfully separate ourselves from the rest of the world.

Exasperation over our struggle in Vietnam should not close our eyes to the fact that we could have other missile crises in the future—different kinds, no doubt, and under different circumstances. But if we are to be successful then, if we are going to preserve our own national security, we will need friends, we will need supporters, we will need countries that believe and respect us and will follow our leadership.

"The importance of placing ourselves in the other country's shoes."

THE FINAL LESSON of the Cuban missile crisis is the importance of placing ourselves in the other country's shoes. During the crisis, President Kennedy spent more time trying to determine the effect of a particular course of action on Khrushchev or the Russians than on any other phase of what he was doing. What guided all his deliberations was an effort not to disgrace Khrushchev, not to humiliate the Soviet Union, not to have them feel they would have to escalate their response because their national security or national interests so committed them.

This was why he was so reluctant to stop and search a Russian ship; this was why he was so opposed to attacking the missile sites. The Russians, he felt, would have to react militarily to such actions on our part.

Thus the initial decision to impose a quarantine rather than to attack; our decision to permit the *Bu-*

charest to pass; our decision to board a non-Russian vessel first; all these and many more were taken with a view to putting pressure on the Soviet Union but not causing a public humiliation.

Miscalculation and misunderstanding and escalation on one side bring a counterresponse. No action is taken against a powerful adversary in a vacuum. A government or people will fail to understand this only at their great peril. For that is how wars begin—wars that no one wants, no one intends, and no one wins.

Each decision that President Kennedy made kept this in mind. Always he asked himself: Can we be sure that Khrushchev understands what we feel to be our vital national interest? Has the Soviet Union had sufficient time to react soberly to a particular step we have taken? All action was judged against that standard—stopping a particular ship, sending low-flying planes, making a public statement.

President Kennedy understood that the Soviet Union did not want war, and they understood that we wished to avoid armed conflict. Thus, if hostilities were to come, it would be either because our national interests collided—which, because of their limited interests and our purposely limited objectives, seemed unlikely —or because of our failure or their failure to understand the other's objectives.

President Kennedy dedicated himself to making it clear to Khrushchev by word and deed—for both are important—that the U.S. had limited objectives and that we had no interest in accomplishing those objectives by adversely affecting the national security of the Soviet Union or by humiliating her.

Later, he was to say in his speech at American University in June of 1963: "Above all, while defending our own vital interests, nuclear powers must avert those confrontations which bring an adversary to the choice of either a humiliating defeat or a nuclear war."

During our crisis talks, he kept stressing the fact that we would indeed have war if we placed the Soviet Union in a position she believed would adversely affect her national security or such public humiliation that she lost the respect of her own people and countries around the globe. The missiles in Cuba, we felt, vitally concerned our national security, but not that of the Soviet Union.

This fact was ultimately recognized by Khrushchev, and this recognition, I believe, brought about his change in what, up to that time, had been a very adamant position. The President believed from the start that the Soviet Chairman was a rational, intelligent man who, if given sufficient time and shown our determination, would alter his position. But there was always the chance of error, of mistake, miscalculation, or misunderstanding, and President Kennedy was committed to doing everything possible to lessen that chance on our side.

The possibility of the destruction of mankind was always in his mind. Someone once said that World War Three would be fought with atomic weapons and the next war with sticks and stones.

As mentioned before, Barbara Tuchman's *The Guns of August* had made a great impression on the President. "I am not going to follow a course which will allow anyone to write a comparable book about this time, *The Missiles of October*," he said to me that Saturday night, October 26. "If anybody is around to write after this, they are going to understand that we made every effort to find peace and every effort to give our adversary room to move. I am not going to push the Russians an inch beyond what is necessary."

After it was finished, he made no statement attempting to take credit for himself or for the Administration for what had occurred. He instructed all members of the Ex Comm and government that no interview should be given, no statement made, which would claim any kind of victory. He respected Khrushchev for properly determining what was in his own country's interest and what was in the interest of mankind. If it was a triumph, it was a triumph for the next generation and not for any particular government or people.

At the outbreak of the First World War the ex-Chancellor of Germany, Prince von Bülow, said to his successor, "How did it all happen?" "Ah, if only we knew," was the reply.

NOTE

It was Senator Kennedy's intention to add a discussion of the basic ethical question involved: what, if any, circumstance or justification gives this government or any government the moral right to bring its people and possibly all people under the shadow of nuclear destruction? He wrote this book in the summer and fall of 1967 on the basis of his personal diaries and recollections, but never had an opportunity to rewrite or complete it.

THEODORE C. SORENSEN

Afterword

BY RICHARD E. NEUSTADT AND GRAHAM T. ALLISON

*T*HE CUBAN MISSILE CRISIS is important at three distinct levels. First, the crisis stands for something central in our time: we live under the cloud of nuclear weapons. Our imaginations have been dulled by metaphors. But it is nonetheless true that today men control the power to destroy mankind. Second, this crisis is a microcosm of problems of the modern American Presidency. Crises tend to highlight the basic characteristics of an institution. The Cuban missile crisis does this for a number of dilemmas in our governmental system. Third, this event poses dramatically a central constitutional issue for the 1970's: namely, the respective roles of President and Congress in making war. During the Cuban missile crisis, the President alone decided and disposed. Two hours before his decision was announced to the world, Congressional leaders were *informed* that the United States was responding to the Soviet missiles with a naval quarantine.

Comparable presidential authority has been asserted even where there is no direct threat of nuclear war. Relying on the minimal Congressional consent represented by the Tonkin Gulf Resolution, President Johnson committed American ground forces to what has become the longest war in our history. Relying on inherent powers of the Commander in Chief to protect American troops, President Nixon ordered an invasion of Cambodia. The Constitution calls for Congress to declare war. But in these cases—as with others in our history—Congress has not played a commensurate role. The result is a great argument over the

Afterword

constitutional balance in warmaking. The missile crisis offers some perspective on this argument.

THE NUCLEAR PARADOX

In October 1962, President John Kennedy chose a path of action that, in his judgment, entailed a one-in-three chance of nuclear war.* Given the potential consequences, how could he possibly have chosen this course? Robert Kennedy participated in the choice, approved of it, and took pride in the Administration's performance. It is a mark of both the man and the times that five years later, recording his memoir of the crisis, he came to wonder about the question: "What, if any, circumstance or justification gives this government or any government the moral right to bring its people and possibly all people under the shadow of nuclear destruction?"

That the United States and Soviet Union could engage in a nuclear war which would effectively destroy both societies (and much of the rest of the world) is a plain but incredible fact about contemporary life. We are now twenty-six years into the nuclear age. For more than a decade, the Soviet Union has been capable of destroying millions of Americans. Yet no war has come. Today who can believe that such a war could come?

How does our nuclear era differ from previous periods? Students of international politics have identified three qualitatively new aspects of the threat and use of force in an era of thermonuclear weapons and ballistic missiles. First, the magnitude of destructive power of thermonuclear weapons is unparalleled. Previously, men have

* According to Theodore Sorensen, "The odds that the Soviets would go all the way to war, he [John Kennedy] later said, seemed to him then 'somewhere between one out of three and even'" (*Kennedy* [New York: Harper & Row, 1965], p. 705).

destroyed men by bullets and bombs. Today, the explosive power of a single thermonuclear bomb exceeds the total explosive power of all bombs used in all wars of the past, including those of this century. Second, the suddenness and swiftness with which mass destruction can be inflicted has no precedent. Surprise attacks are not new. But today no point on the globe lies more than minutes away from annihilation by a ballistic missile. Third, because of the first two factors, the meaning has been taken out of "victory" in war. As recently as 1945, victory consisted of disarming the enemy, after which the victor could determine the fate of the vanquished. Today, it is not necessary to defeat a nation's armies before disposing of its citizens. The use of arms and soldiers to prevent occupation of one's country is no longer sufficient to guarantee its citizens against destruction.

In personal and societal terms, what these new conditions mean was stated starkly by one of the participants in the missile crisis, Robert McNamara. The Secretary of Defense testified to Congress in 1964: "In the first hour [of all-out nuclear war] one hundred million Americans and one hundred million Russians would be killed."

Such hard physical facts are difficult to accept. But even less acceptable, given these conditions, is that nations could *choose* war. The United States and the Soviet Union now live in a world of "mutual superiority," that is, mutual capability to do unacceptable damage to the other (even after having been struck first). Under such conditions, could the Soviet Union or United States initiate a nuclear war, killing millions of the opponents and suffering in retaliation the destruction of millions of its own citizens? As Thomas Schelling has written, "there is just no foreseeable route by which the United States and Soviet Union could become involved in a major nuclear war." Since choosing nuclear war would be, in effect, to choose mutual homicide,

Afterword

President Dwight D. Eisenhower concluded, "War is impossible. . . . there is no alternative to peace."

Many observers find in the Cuban missile crisis confirmation for their belief that nuclear war is impossible. The crisis did not explode. The leaders who lived through that crisis felt what it was like to peer over the precipice. Since that time, both governments have exercised extraordinary caution about all things nuclear, circumventing interests in order to avoid fundamental clashes, cooling conflicts that might erupt, and discouraging the nuclear programs of other nations. Today, nuclear war between the United States and the Soviet Union *is* very unlikely.

But no event demonstrates more clearly than the missile crisis that with respect to nuclear war there is an awesome crack between *unlikelihood* and *impossibility*. Though many accounts of the crisis downgrade its risks (reflecting the widespread inability to believe that nuclear war could occur), Robert Kennedy's memoir documents how close the United States and the Soviet Union came to making the impossible happen.

How could nuclear war have emerged from this crisis? An alarming number of plausible paths branch off the actual course of events and end in nuclear war. In order to aid the reader, we will summarize what happened in the form of a scenario and then spell out one of the paths that could have led to war. Actual events are represented by eight steps.

1. The Soviet Union puts missiles in Cuba clandestinely (September 6, 1962).

2. U.S. U-2 flight discovers Soviet missiles (October 14, 1962).

3. President Kennedy initiates a public confrontation by announcing to the world the Soviet action, demanding Soviet withdrawal of the missiles, ordering a U.S. quarantine of Soviet weapon shipments to Cuba, putting U.S.

strategic forces on full alert, and warning the Soviet Union that any missile launched from Cuba would be regarded as a Soviet missile and met with a full retaliatory response (October 22).

4. Khrushchev orders Soviet strategic forces to full alert and threatens to sink U.S. ships if they interfere with Soviet ships en route to Cuba (October 24).

5. Soviet ships stop short of the U.S. quarantine line (October 25).

6. Khrushchev letter offers withdrawal of Soviet missiles in return for U.S. noninvasion pledge (October 26), followed by a second Khrushchev letter demanding U.S. withdrawal of Turkish missiles for Soviet withdrawal of Cuban missiles (October 27).

7. U.S. responds affirmatively to first Khrushchev letter but warns that if missiles are not withdrawn by Sunday, October 28, invasion or air strike will follow Monday or Tuesday (October 27).

8. Khrushchev announces withdrawal of the missiles (October 28).

Perhaps the most obvious scenario by which nuclear war might have emerged from the sequence follows the actual course of events through step seven, but then proceeds:

(8) Khrushchev reiterates that any attack on Soviet missiles and personnel in Cuba will be met with a full Soviet retaliatory response (October 28).

(9) U.S. "surgical" air strike against Soviet missiles (destroying all operational ballistic missiles and killing a limited number of Soviet personnel) (October 30).

(10) Soviet medium-range ballistic missiles attack U.S. missiles in Turkey (destroying all ballistic missiles and killing a small number of Americans) (October 31).

(11) In accord with obligations under the NATO treaty, U.S. medium-range missiles in Europe attack bases

in the Soviet Union from which missiles that attacked the Turkish bases were launched (October 31).

(12) Soviet Union, fearing additional U.S. attacks on its limited number of ICBMs, attacks the U.S. (November 1).

(13) U.S. ICBMs attack the Soviet Union (November 1).

Alternative scenarios leading to nuclear war could start with the firing of Soviet missiles in Cuba or the sinking of a ship. Moreover, a large number of potential "accidents" might have triggered nuclear war, for example, the Soviet downing of a U-2 aircraft on Saturday, October 27, nearly precipitated an American attack on Soviet surface-to-air missiles. Robert Kennedy identifies at least five other incidents that could have served as a nuclear fuse.

Given the many possible nuclear dead ends that branch off the path of confrontation, why did President Kennedy start down this path? Need Soviet recklessness have been matched in kind? Could Kennedy not have accepted their missiles in Cuba and announced to the world that Russian roulette was a game he would not play? What consequences of the Soviet move could justify his choice, instead, of countermoves that ran so high a risk of holocaust?

The mind searches for easy answers. Perhaps the President had no alternative. There is more than humor in Robert Kennedy's reply to his brother when, halfway down the confrontation track, John Kennedy wondered how they had ever started: "If you hadn't acted, you would have been impeached." No doubt, the President felt personally challenged. But none of these considerations suggest why he felt that such a choice was tolerable, rational, justifiable.

Answers to that question go to the heart of what we have termed the nuclear paradox: *in a world of mutual superiority, neither nation can win a nuclear war, but each must be willing to risk losing.* Consider each clause of the paradox. First, if war comes, both nations lose. There is no value for which rational leaders could reasonably choose the deaths of millions of their own citizens. In that sense, conditions make a President Kennedy and a Chairman Khrushchev partners in a game of preventing mutual disaster. But this is the condition of both nations and the leaders of both nations know it. Thus if one nation is unwilling to risk waging (losing) a nuclear war, the opponent can win any objective by threatening to take the dispute to that level of risk. In order to be able to preserve certain values, the leaders must be willing not to choose destruction, but nonetheless to choose the risk of destruction.

It could be argued that, despite the risk inherent in the course of action President Kennedy chose, any other course would have meant greater risk. If, rather than challenging Khrushchev and demanding withdrawal of the missiles, he simply had accepted Khrushchev's move and minimized its importance, what would the consequences have been? First, the "rules of the precarious status quo" that the President referred to during the crisis would have been seriously jeopardized. Outside the Ex Comm conference room in the State Department there was a sign: "In the nuclear age, superpowers make war like porcupines make love—carefully." Kennedy had tried to establish rules that would prevent either nation from miscalculating the other's vital interests and stumbling by misunderstanding into a confrontation from which neither could retreat. If Khrushchev's most serious infraction of these rules were disregarded, the rules would wear away. Second, the Soviet action constituted the most blatant breach of confidence and trust between Khrushchev and Kennedy. Kennedy had announced in the firmest terms possible that the United States would not tolerate Soviet offensive weapons in Cuba. Khrushchev had assured Kennedy that the Soviet

Union would not place missiles in Cuba. After these promises—both public and private—Khrushchev proceeded to do what he had forsworn. If Khrushchev could so miscalculate the President's meaning and mettle, what line could the President draw that Khrushchev would respect? Third, the Soviet emplacement of missiles in Cuba seemed tied to the Soviet plan for action on Berlin. If the United States simply accepted Soviet action in Cuba, it might not be able to persuade the Soviet Union that it was willing to run the risk of nuclear war to preserve Berlin. Finally, the fact that the Soviet leaders had taken such a reckless step suggested that they did not appreciate how dangerous and precarious were relations between nuclear superpowers. Until this was rooted in their minds, they might continue to take actions that ran significant risks of nuclear war, hoping that the United States would yield rather than accept such risks. Though dangerous, Cuba was nonetheless likely to be more manageable than Berlin, or the crisis after Berlin. Nowhere outside the continental United States did we enjoy such a comparative advantage in conventional forces.

Thus President Kennedy might have justified his action as the lesser of risky alternatives. To the question that had begun to trouble Robert Kennedy—What right or justification is there for bringing people under such risk?—he might have answered: I did not bring people under such risk; this is simply our present condition. But Robert Kennedy's question seems to ask: what justification can there be for tolerating that condition? What seems immoral and, indeed, irrational and intolerable is that technology forces fallible human beings to make choices about life and death for hundreds of millions of other human beings. Would any reasonable man choose to live in such a world? The nuclear paradox cannot be denied. But can it be accepted?

One way to avoid the bite of Robert Kennedy's question lies in wishing risks away, discounting by denying them, or closing eyes to them. The authors of this Afterword have heard a lot of wishing done by government officials in the aftermath of Cuba. Some men near the Ex Comm but not of it—mainly military officers advising in subordinate capacities—have argued strongly that from the moment President Kennedy went on the air to publicize American awareness and reaction there was never a substantial risk of nuclear war. Faced by our obvious superiority, both strategic and tactical, the Russians, being rational, were bound to retreat. What then of Kennedy's perception, movingly attested by his brother, that the risk of holocaust was real? These officers dismiss it as "flap in the White House." Other men, including some who sat around the table, now persuade themselves instead that "toughness pays." If there was risk, it lasted only until our destroyers, troops, and aircraft were deployed in the Atlantic and in Florida. Thereafter, while we held firm, Khrushchev had no alternative except to turn his ships around and stop construction at the missile sites.

Such "lessons" offer comfort, but they share a flaw. It lies in the assumption that the Soviet rulers were at once cool calculators, reasoning from all the evidence at *our* disposal, and assured controllers, orchestrating every act of their bureaucracies. As Robert Kennedy informs us, this is an assumption that the President resisted. His resistance accounts for the "flap" at the White House.

What Kennedy appears to have believed is that Khrushchev might be a ruler somewhat like himself, beset by uncertainties in seeking evidence and weighing it, likely to misjudge its meaning in another country's context, susceptible to human imperfections of emotion and fatigue, plagued also by the bureaucratic imperfections of communication and control. Khrushchev's long message on Friday night, October 26, seems powerfully to have reinforced this presidential point of view, adding to White House concern about a third week of crisis. If the Russians held their course for a mere seventy-two hours, we would have to escalate a step, probably by bombing Cuban sites. In logic, they should then bomb Turkish sites. Then we . . . ; then they. . . . The third step is what evidently haunted Kennedy. If Khrushchev's capability to calculate and to control was something like his own, then neither's might suffice to guide them both through that third step without holocaust.

NEW CHECKS AND BALANCES

In warmaking, the Constitution contemplated enforced collaboration between the President and his fellow politicians on Capitol Hill. In practice, as the missile crisis illustrates, a strong role for Congress is by no means assured. This does not mean, however, that Presidents act in isolation. Any modern President stands at the center of a watchful circle with whose members he cannot help but consult. Today, indeed, he is more dependent on Executive officials for advice as well as execution than our Constitution makers could have anticipated two centuries ago.

New checks and balances replace the old. There is, however, one extraordinary difference: the old circle was supposedly comprised of men who owed their places to elections, who themselves had experienced the risks of nomination and electioneering. Political accountability conferred on each, firsthand, legitimacy as an agent of the people. Indeed, our Constitution's democratic element consisted mainly in reserving to these men the great decisions on the use of force. By contrast, the new circle is appointive or co-optive: congressmen may enter it and so may private citizens when their service as surrogates is wanted by a President. But mostly, and continuously, those assured an entry are the President's own appointees: department heads, Chiefs of Staff, White House aides, and others whose institutional positions or personal relations make their presence virtual necessities for him. As this implies, they are by no means "mere" subordinates. He is no freer than he would have been with Congress to ignore them. But neither are they colleagues in the sense of sharing either his legitimacy or accountability. Nowadays those rest with him alone.

Consider again the group that made fundamental choices for the United States during the missile crisis. Who were the members?

First, there was the President as constitutional Commander in Chief, nationally elected. No other elective officer was so involved (save the Vice-President, an appropriately attentive listener). No member of the Senate or House stands astride the action channel for decisions on nuclear war. None is consulted unless the President so chooses as a matter of discretion. In October 1962, Congress remained ignorant of the Soviet missiles in Cuba during the first week of Ex Comm deliberations. Only on October 22, two hours before his broadcast to the world, did the President assemble the leaders of both houses, advise them of the missiles, and inform them that he had decided to respond with a naval quarantine. The Congressional leaders disagreed strongly with the course the President had chosen. Senator Fulbright in particular urged that the United States respond more forcefully. Senator Russell stated that "he could not live with himself if he did not say in the strongest possible terms how important it was that we act with greater strength." The Senators insisted that the record show they had been informed, not consulted. But Congressional objections had no effect at that point. Nor was any member of Congress deeply involved in subsequent decisions during the week that followed.

Second, there were several men whose institutional positions made them unavoidable parties to any major choice about nuclear war: the Secretary of Defense, the Secretary of State, the Director of the Central Intelligence Agency, the Chairman of the Joint Chiefs of Staff, and the White House Assistant for National Security Affairs. Why were these men involved *of necessity?* Because each had a portion of the wherewithal for action. As the President considered possible military moves, who could specify the spectrum of feasible options except the Joint Chiefs of Staff and their subordinates? When the President chose blockade, no one but the Secretary of Defense had both the authority and the information to oversee its implementation. Who told the President about the presence of Soviet missiles in Cuba? His Assistant for National Security Affairs, McGeorge Bundy. (Indeed, Bundy chose not to tell him on the evening of Monday, October 15, when the CIA informed Bundy of this fact, but rather to let the President get a good night's sleep on the fifteenth before telling him on the morning of the sixteenth.) Bundy learned about the missiles from the CIA; the Director of the CIA, John McCone, and the machine under him served as the "eyes and ears" of the U.S. government in keeping abreast of developments in Cuba. The need for information, analysis, and assistance in implementation meant that Deputy Secretaries and even the relevant Assistant Secretaries also were included, as, for example, Paul Nitze of Defense.

Third, there were the President's men: his brother and campaign manager, the Attorney General, and his Special Counsel, Theodore Sorensen. Sorensen had joined JFK when he went to the Senate in 1953 and ever since had been among his closest personal and programmatic advisers as well as his principal speechwriter. The President depended on Sorensen for more than words in speeches. Sorensen, and even more Robert Kennedy, helped John

Kennedy assess the full spectrum of his responsibilities as President. Having depended on the national security apparatus alone in making the fateful choice about the Bay of Pigs, Kennedy insisted thereafter that no major national security decision be made without including RFK and Sorensen in the process.

Fourth, there were the surrogates, some of them officials, some from private life. Dean Acheson was a former Secretary of State; Robert Lovett, a former Secretary of Defense. Both had served the Truman Administration, Lovett as a Republican. They were involved because the President happened to value their judgment and also because he knew that others valued their judgment—especially in the "bipartisan foreign policy establishment"—on Capitol Hill and off. Adlai Stevenson, Ambassador to the United Nations, can be counted of their number since his position as a former Democratic presidential candidate and liberal outweighed the importance of his official role. The presence of the Secretary of the Treasury, Douglas Dillon, attests not only to the weight accorded his department in matters of foreign affairs—a vital if half-hidden feature of our government—but also to his representative character as Eisenhower's former Undersecretary of State.

The importance of the individuals in the circle becomes clear as one reflects on the extraordinary role they played. Decisions passed through the President's hand but were not simply the product of his mind alone. Both the definition of the issue and the choice of the U.S. response *emerged* from deliberations of the group. Robert Kennedy's account is suggestive, both about individual perceptions and preferences, and about the process by which the group came to the blockade.*

On the morning of Tuesday, October 16, McGeorge

---

* Other accounts supplement his discussion. For these accounts, see p. 179. In the paragraphs that follow, we have drawn on some of them.

Bundy went to the President's living quarters with the message: "Mr. President, there is now hard photographic evidence that the Russians have offensive missiles in Cuba." Much has been made of Kennedy's "expression of surprise." But "surprise" fails to capture the character of his initial reaction. Rather it was one of startled anger, most adequately conveyed by the exclamation: "He can't do that to *me!*" That exclamation in this context was triple-barreled. First, in terms of the President's attention and priorities at the moment, Khrushchev had chosen the most unhelpful act of all. In a highly sensitive domestic political context—less than two years after the Bay of Pigs, less than two months before mid-term elections—where his opponents demanded action against Soviet interests in Cuba, Kennedy was following a policy of reason and responsibility. In support of that policy, he had drawn a distinction between "defensive" and "offensive" weapons, staked his full presidential authority on the flat statement that the Soviets were not placing offensive weapons in Cuba, and warned unambiguously that offensive missiles would not be tolerated. Second, the main thrust of his Administration's policy toward the Soviet Union had been aimed at relaxing tension and building trust through trust. At considerable political cost, he was attempting to leash the anti-Communist cold warriors and to educate officials, as well as the public, out of prevailing devil theories of Soviet Communism. He and his closest advisers had made considerable effort to guarantee that all communication between the President and the Chairman would be straightforward and accurate. Contact had been made; Khrushchev was reciprocating; mutual confidence was growing. As part of this exchange, Khrushchev had assured the President through the most direct and personal channels that he was aware of Kennedy's domestic problem and would do nothing to complicate it. Specifically, Khrushchev had given the President solemn assurances that the Soviet Union would not put offensive missiles in Cuba. But then this—the Chairman had *lied* to the President.* Third, Khrushchev's action challenged the President personally. Did he, John F. Kennedy, have the courage in the crunch to start down a path with significant probability of nuclear war? If not, Khrushchev would win this round. More important, he would gain confidence that he could win the next as well—simply by forcing Kennedy to choose between a nuclear path and acquiescense. Kennedy had worried, both after the Bay of Pigs and after his Vienna meeting with Khrushchev, that the Chairman might have misjudged his mettle. This time Kennedy was determined to stand fast. The nonforcible paths—avoiding military measures, resorting instead to diplomacy—could not have been less relevant to *his* problem.

These two paths—"doing nothing" or "taking a diplomatic approach" as the alternatives were labeled in the Ex Comm—were the solutions advocated by two of his principal advisers. For Secretary of Defense McNamara, the missiles raised a specter of nuclear war. He first framed the issue as a straightforward strategic problem. To understand the issue, one had to grasp two obvious but difficult points. First, the missiles in Cuba represented an inevitable occurrence: narrowing of the missile gap between the United States and U.S.S.R. It simply happened sooner rather than later. Second, the United States could accept this occurrence since its consequences were minor: seven to one missile "superiority," one to one missile "equality," one to seven missile "inferiority"—the three positions are identical. What was identical was the unacceptability of

---

* According to memoirs attributed to Khrushchev, "Our goal was . . . to keep the Americans from invading Cuba, and, to that end, we wanted to make them think twice by confronting them with our missiles" (*Khrushchev Remembers* [Boston: Little, Brown, 1970], p. 496). This account avoids any discussion of the deception involved.

the American casualties that could be inflicted from any of the three. McNamara's statement of this argument at the first meeting of the Ex Comm was summed up in a phrase, "a missile is a missile." "It makes no great difference," he maintained, "whether you were killed by a missile from the Soviet Union or Cuba." The implication was clear. The United States should not initiate a crisis with the Soviet Union, risking a significant probability of nuclear war, over an occurrence that had such small strategic implications.

The perceptions of McGeorge Bundy are difficult to reconstruct. He too seems to have been impressed primarily by the potential in the proposed military actions for escalation to nuclear war, since initially he was the advocate of a diplomatic approach. Several forms of diplomatic approach were outlined, but Bundy argued most persuasively for either confronting Soviet Foreign Minister Gromyko with the evidence and demanding withdrawal, or directly approaching Khrushchev in a similar manner. As he pointed out, this approach would give Khrushchev an opportunity to withdraw the missiles quietly, without humiliation. It might avoid any confrontation whatever. It reduced the length of time this secret would have to stay bottled up inside our government. Moreover, Bundy argued, consider the alternatives—each called for springing the discovery on Khrushchev when announcing to the American people and the world the chosen course of action. This amounted to a suspension of the rules of diplomacy. To make this a public issue engaging Khrushchev's and the Soviets' prestige in the eyes of the world, before trying traditional diplomatic channels, would be at best shortsighted. Finally, in terms of the argument that became the touchstone of these deliberations, a diplomatic approach closed no other options. If Khrushchev refused or delayed, an alternative could then be publicly announced, and the Administration would be shielded from criticisms that it had provoked the public confrontation without first attempting diplomatic negotiations.

Bundy's argument was powerful. But the tone of the argument and the fact that later in the week he became an advocate of the air strike leaves some doubt about his "real" reaction. Was he laboring under his acknowledged burden of responsibility in the fiasco at the Bay of Pigs? Was he playing the role of devil's advocate in order to make the President probe his own initial reaction? As Bundy summarized his own reaction, "I almost deliberately stayed in the minority. I felt that it was very important to keep the President's choices open."

Robert Kennedy saw the political wall against which Khrushchev had backed his brother. But he found himself hemmed in by two additional barriers as well. First, like McNamara, he was haunted by the prospect of nuclear doom. Was Khrushchev going to force the President into an insane act? Second, more than any other member of the group, he saw a vital issue posed by the traditions and moral position of the United States. Was his brother going to blacken the name of the United States in the pages of history? Recall his scribbled note at the first meeting of the Ex Comm: "I now know how Tojo felt when he was planning Pearl Harbor." From the outset he probed for an alternative to the air strike.

The initial reaction of Theodore Sorensen fell somewhere between the President and his brother. Like the President, Sorensen felt the sting of betrayal. If the President had been the architect of the policy the missiles punctured, Sorensen was the draftsman. Khrushchev's deceitful move demanded a strong countermove. But like Robert Kennedy, Sorensen feared lest shock and disgrace lead to disaster. Chosen by the President to be his primary reporter on the discussions in the Ex Comm, Sorensen guarded against becoming an advocate. Instead, in the Ex Comm he conceived his role to be one of assisting in "prodding, questioning, eliciting argument and alternatives and keeping discussion concrete and moving ahead." But because his memos posed for the President the issues, arguments, and questions, his personal reactions mattered.

To the Joint Chiefs of Staff the issue was clear. *Now* was the time to do the job for which they had been preparing contingency plans. The Bay of Pigs was badly done; this round would not be. The missiles provided the *occasion* to deal with the issue for which they were prepared: ridding the Western Hemisphere of Castro's Communism. The security of the United States required a massive air strike, leading to an invasion and the overthrow of Castro. As General Maxwell Taylor, Chairman of the Joint Chiefs, recalls: "I was a twofold Hawk from start to finish, first as a spokesman for the Joint Chiefs of Staff, secondly from personal conviction." * While Taylor argued his position carefully, two of the Chiefs advocated military action with an abandon that amazed other members of the Ex Comm. As Robert Kennedy notes, after Air Force Chief of Staff General Curtis LeMay had argued strongly that a military attack was essential, the President asked what the response of the Russians might be. General LeMay replied: "There would be no reaction." The President was not convinced. As he told White House aide Arthur Schlesinger, Jr. on the day the crisis ended, "An invasion would have been a mistake—a wrong use of our power. But the military are mad. They wanted to do this. It's lucky for us we have McNamara over there."

There were other, more persuasive advocates of military action. Acheson, Nitze, Dillon, and McCone found themselves of like mind. Dean Rusk, the Secretary of State, seems to have leaned in their direction. To this group the overriding issues were two: the security of the United

* Maxwell Taylor, *Memoirs* (New York: W. W. Norton & Company, forthcoming).

States together with its position of leadership in the Western Hemisphere and Western Europe. The situation permitted little time for deliberation. The Soviet missiles in Cuba were fast becoming an acute danger and should be removed by military action before they become operational. In Acheson's words:

As I saw it at the time, and still believe, the decision to resort to the blockade was a decision to postpone the issue at the expense of time within which the nuclear weapons might be made operational. The Soviet Union did not need to bring any more weapons into Cuba . . . the nuclear weapons already there . . . were capable of killing eighty million Americans. That was enough.*

As Nitze maintained, when starting down a path that might lead to nuclear war, any man with a responsible regard for the lives of American citizens had to distinguish sharply between the consequences of war before and after those missiles became operational.

Thus the Soviet missiles in Cuba posed no single issue. The men who gathered at the pinnacle of the U.S. government perceived many facets of quite different issues. And in spite of efforts to classify these men simply as "hawks" and "doves"—metaphors coined during this crisis —their initial reactions were much more diverse than the metaphors suggest. The process by which the blockade emerged from these initial reactions and preferences is a story of the most subtle and intricate probing, pulling and hauling, leading, guiding and spurring. Even with the aid of Robert Kennedy's account, reconstruction of this process can only be tentative.

Initially the President and most of his advisers wanted a clean, surgical air strike. On the first day of the crisis, when informing Adlai Stevenson of the missiles, the Presi-

* Dean Acheson, "Homage to Plain Dumb Luck," *Esquire*, February, 1969.

dent mentioned only two alternatives: "I suppose the alternatives are to go in by air and wipe them out, or to take other steps to render them inoperable." At the end of the week a sizeable minority still favored an air strike. As Robert Kennedy once told an interviewer: "The fourteen people involved were very significant. . . . If six of them had been President of the U.S., I think that the world might have been blown up." What prevented the air strike was a fortuitous coincidence of a number of factors, the absence of any one of which might have permitted that option to prevail.

First, McNamara's vision of holocaust set him firmly against the air strike. His initial attempt to frame the issue in strategic terms struck Kennedy as particularly inappropriate. Once McNamara realized that a strong response was required, however, he and his deputy Gilpatric chose the blockade as a fallback. When the Secretary of Defense—whose department had the action, whose reputation in the Cabinet was unequaled, in whom the President demonstrated full confidence—marshalled the arguments for the blockade and refused to be moved, the blockade became a formidable alternative.

Second, Robert Kennedy pressed the "Tojo" analogy. His arguments against the air strike on moral grounds struck a chord in the President. Moreover, once those arguments had been stated so forcefully, the President scarcely could have followed his initial preference without seeming to become what RFK had condemned.

The President learned of the missiles on Tuesday morning. On Wednesday morning, in order to mask the discovery from the Russians, he flew to Connecticut to keep a campaign commitment, leaving his brother as the unofficial chairman of the group. By the time the President returned on Wednesday evening, a critical third piece had been added to the picture. McNamara had presented his argument for the blockade. Robert Kennedy and Sorensen had joined him. A powerful coalition of the advisers in whom the President had the greatest confidence, and with whom he was personally most compatible, had emerged.

Fourth, the coalition that had formed behind the President's initial preference gave him reason to pause. Who supported the air strike—the Chiefs, McCone, and Acheson for instance—counted as much as *how* they supported it.

Fifth, a piece of inaccurate information, which no one probed, permitted the blockade advocates to fuel (potential) uncertainties in the President's mind. When the President returned to Washington Wednesday evening, RFK and Sorensen met him at the airport. Sorensen gave the President a four-page memorandum outlining the areas of agreement and disagreement. The strongest argument was that the air strike simply could not be surgical. After a day of prodding and questioning, the Air Force had asserted that it could not guarantee the success of a surgical air strike limited to the missiles alone.

Thursday evening, the President convened the Ex Comm at the White House. He declared his tentative choice of the blockade and directed that preparations be made to put it into effect by Monday morning. Though he raised a question about the possibility of a surgical air strike subsequently, he seems to have accepted the experts' opinion that this was no live option. (Acceptance of this estimate suggests that he may have learned the lesson of the Bay of Pigs—"Never rely on experts"—less well than he supposed.) This information seems to have been incorrect. During the second week of the crisis, civilian analysts examined the surgical air strike option, asserted that with suitable modification of Air Force plans this option could be chosen with high confidence, and thus added it to the list of possible choices for the end of the second week. Why no one probed the initial estimates earlier remains an interesting question.

The decision to blockade thus emerged as a collage. Its pieces included the initial decision by the President that something forceful had to be done; the resistance of Robert Kennedy, McNamara, and Sorensen to the air strike; the relative distance between the President and the air strike advocates; and a probably inaccurate piece of information.*

A DILEMMA OF GOVERNANCE

The process of decision in this case illustrates a set of checks and balances almost unmentioned by our Constitution. A President and his top-level associates are mutually dependent. But their needs of one another can be incompatible. Rarely do they serve each other to their mutual satisfaction. Robert Kennedy's account suggests that in the Cuban missile crisis satisfaction was indeed obtained by both. A careful reading will suggest, however, the fragility of this result. It is not to be taken for granted.

What President Kennedy needed from executive officialdom is plain in his brother's story. He needed information, analysis, and control to match his own unshared and now unshareable responsibility. In retrospect he seems to have received enough of each, but only just, and only by extraordinary effort on his own part and on that of his most intimate associates. The U-2 photographs were taken in the nick of time for him; our aircraft lined up wing-to-wing were not dispersed until he intervened; his agent McNamara never did succeed in wresting from the Navy

---

* The preceding paragraphs are adapted from Graham T. Allison, *Essence of Decision: Explaining the Cuban Missile Crisis* (Boston: Little, Brown, 1971).

full control over its ships, and only Soviet caution saved him from the consequences of an Air Force pilot's fix on the wrong star. What he needed, evidently, was information building up from small details and control reaching down to small decisions in the depths of every relevant department. These were his needs because the country and its future depended so heavily on his judgment.

What top officials needed from the President is also plain in RFK's account of the Ex Comm. They needed a forum for discussion, a referee for arguments, assurance of a hearing, and a judgment on disputes. Their jurisdictions were at once divided and entangled. The Secretaries of Defense and State, the military services, the CIA, our missions at the United Nations and at NATO all had roles to play, but these required each to share the stage with all the rest. None could act alone. And their perspectives were parochial (at least in in some degree). The Air Force saw the interest of the nation—and its options—in terms diametrically opposed to those of our Ambassador at the United Nations. The Secretary of Defense weighed up MRBMs in Cuba and derived a different balance than his State Department counterparts: he emphasized deterrence while they emphasized diplomacy. Robert Kennedy and Dean Acheson differed over the lessons of history and the lessons that U.S. action in this case would teach the future.

In hindsight, the invention of the Ex Comm and its improvised procedures (including sessions separate from the President) gave men like these the very things they needed, under circumstances bound to minimize parochialism, strengthening their sense of common service to the top. But JFK's contrivance of a special hearing for the Air Force case before he ruled against an air strike at the start suggests that the Ex Comm had its limits as a forum, also as a court-of-last-resort. And in the second week of crisis there were signs aplenty that the third week might have witnessed something close to an explosion by harassed, frustrated, shut-out bureaucrats below the top. If so, their weary seniors, strained by thirteen days, scarcely could have contained them. As a means to meet the needs of second-level men, the Ex Comm was a travesty. Yet by the sixteenth day their needs would have been paramount. They would have had to mount the military operations and the corollary diplomatic actions.

Thirteen Days does not have much to say about the needs and frustrations of subordinate officials. It is a personal memoir and its author viewed the scene from a position close to the top. But the authors of this Afterword have heard in vivid detail the complaints of those below, also their hopes and plans. As one of us once told a Senate subcommittee:

One can already see in these two weeks (of missile crisis) frustration rising at official levels. The . . . needs of officials in their own lives and work would have proven very intense indeed over a month. Two weeks were quite enough to build up great concern about being left out of things. At the same time, action officers were finding no department heads to take their issues to. . . . Then add to these psychological and operating troubles . . . that there evidently was beginning to be a proliferation of ad hoc subcommittees under the Ex Comm—and I think I can tell you what would have happened in the course of a month. . . .

Officials would have fastened on to these new subcommittees as a way of getting all the secondary issues raised up and also as a way of getting into the act of top decisionmaking. [Soon] . . . there would have been two or three levels of committees. They would have been in existence long enough so that people had vested rights. . . . You would have had an Operations Coordinating Board structure magnified and growing like Topsy. Then suppose the whole thing had evolved successfully. The

President would . . . be faced with having to destroy the . . . [structure] . . . in order to get back some flexibility.*

As this suggests, the same forces that shape presidential needs also shape the needs of bureaucrats, but in different ways. Well before the Soviets achieved an ICBM capability, the place of change in our own weaponry, combined with our wide-ranging economic and political endeavors overseas, was mixing up the jurisdictions of all agencies with roles to play, or claim, in national security: mingling operations along programmatic lines, cutting across vertical lines of authority, breaching the neat boxes on organizational charts. Defense, State, CIA, AID, Treasury, together with the President's Executive Office staffs, came to form a single complex—a national security complex, tied together by an intricate network of program and staff interrelationships in Washington and in the field. The Atomic Energy Commission, the Arms Control and Disarmament Agency, and USIA are also in the complex; others lurk nearby, tied in to a degree, as, for example, Commerce.

As early as the National Security Act of 1947, we formally acknowledged the close ties of foreign, military, economic policy; these ties had been rendered very plain by World War II experience. But in pre–Korean War years when the Marshall Plan was on its own, when CIA was new, when military aid programs were hardly heard of, while atom bombs were ours alone, and military budgets stood at under $15 billion, a Secretary of Defense could forbid contacts between Pentagon and State at any level lower than his own, and, within limits, could enforce his ban. That happened no longer ago than 1949. In bureaucratic terms it is as remote as the Stone Age.

* U.S., Congress, Senate, Subcommittee on National Security Staffing and Operations, 88th Cong., 1st sess., *Hearings,* Part I, Testimony of Richard E. Neustadt, March 11, 1963, p. 97.

While operations now have been entangled inextricably, our formal organizations and their statutory powers and the jurisdictions of Congressional committees remain much as ever: distinct, disparate, dispersed. Our personnel systems are equally dispersed. In the national security complex alone, we have at least seven separate professional career systems—military included—along with the general civil service, which to most intents and purposes is departmentalized.

These days few staffs in any agency can do their work alone without active support or at least passive acquiescence from staffs outside, in other agencies, often many others. Yet no one agency, no personnel system is the effective boss of any other; no one staff owes effective loyalty to the others. By and large, the stakes which move men's loyalties—whether purpose, prestige, power, or promotion—run to one's own program, one's own career system, along agency lines, not across them.

These developments place premiums on interstaff negotiations, compromise, agreement in the course of everybody's action. This invokes the horrors of committee work: the wastes of time, the earstrain—and the eyestrain—the "papering over" of differences, the search for lowest common denominators of agreement. But given the realities of programming and operations, interagency negotiation cannot be avoided. To "kill" committees is at most to drive them underground. Officials have to find at best an informal equivalent. What else are they to do?

One other thing they can do is push their pet issues up for argument and settlement at higher levels. Once started on this course, there is no very satisfactory place to stop short of the White House. In logic and in law, only the Presidency stands somewhat above all agencies, all personnel systems, all staffs. Here one can hope to gain decisions as definitive as our system permits; Congressional committees may be able to supplant them, special pleaders may be able to reverse them, foot draggers may be able to subvert them—even so, they are the surest thing obtainable.

Accordingly, officials urged to show initiative, to quit logrolling in committee, to be vigorous in advocacy, firm in execution, turn toward the White House seeking from it regular, reliable, consistent service as a fixed and constant court of arbitration for the national security complex. This means, of course, a court which knows how courts behave and does not enter cases prematurely.

Their need for such a service is unquestionable and legitimate. To flounder through the mush of "iffy" answers, or evasions; to struggle through the murk of many voices, few directives; to fight without assurance of a referee; to face Capitol Hill without assurance of a buffer; or on the other hand, to clean up after eager amateurs, to repair damage done by ex parte proceedings; to cope with happy thoughts in highest places—these are what officialdom complains of, and with reason. For the work of large-scale enterprises tends to be disrupted by such breaches of "good order" and routine. Not bureaucrats alone but also Presidents have stakes in the effectiveness of the Executive bureaucracy. From any point of view, officials surely are entitled to want White House service in support of their performance.

But if a President should give this service to their satisfaction, what becomes of him? While he sits as the judge of issues brought by others—keeping order, following procedure, filing decisions, clearing dockets—what happens to his personal initiative, his mastery of detail, his search for information, his reach for control? What happens to his own concerns outside the sphere of national security? In short, where is the flexibility he needs to make himself the master of decisions for which he alone remains politically accountable?

To a degree—a large degree—the needs of any President and those of "his" officialdom are incompatible. Rarely can both be served alike. Usually one suffers as the other benefits. The missile crisis seems a rarity in just this sense. But probably it would not seem so had it lasted for another week.*

Since World War II our government has often tried to square the circle of this incompatibility by tinkering with structure. Alternately, efforts have been made to tighten up procedures for official consultation and to loosen their constraints upon the White House. Sometimes efforts of both sorts have been made at once, with contradictory consequences. Each Administration has begun by altering the structure it inherited to cure a "weakness" in its predecessor's practice as observed from the outside or from below. The National Security Council, created by act of Congress in 1947, has been called Secretary of Defense James Forrestal's revenge on Franklin Roosevelt for the latter's quite incurable and sometimes costly tendency to keep all threads in his own hands, or anyway in no one else's. The subordinate committee structure Eisenhower later sponsored—the Planning Board and Operations Coordinating Board—was said to be a cure-all for alleged disorder under Truman. Kennedy's abrupt dismantling of that structure was regarded as essential to unleash the human energies locked up inside its "paper mill." Nixon now "restores" a somewhat comparable structure, ending the "excesses" of the Johnson White House, but he ties it to a presidential staff more formidable in numbers and in jurisdiction than his predecessors ever had employed.

So goes the tinkering with structure. None of it thus far has obviated the uncomfortable fact that Presidents rarely are better served than when officials are frustrated, and vice versa.

---

* The preceding paragraphs are adapted from Neustadt, *op. cit.*

In terms of structure, Kennedy's most sophisticated contribution was his refusal to continue the Ex Comm once the missile crisis passed its peak. Reportedly he saw it as an indispensable piece of machinery for a crisis-time, indispensable because so flexible and so removed from vested rights or interests. Its use at any other time would vitiate those qualities. Thus he ordered it disbanded, to the dismay of some members, and the very term "Ex Comm" was barred from current use. In this, although not consciously, he followed Truman's practice at the outbreak of the Korean War.

Kennedy's decision to disband the Ex Comm is expressive of the underlying dilemma. There appear to be no ways whereby a President can be assured routinely, at all times and places, of the information and control he needs while simultaneously assuring to officials the hearings, the due process, the appeals, and the forbearance they require of the White House. Even at the farthest remove from routine, the missile crisis above all, these two assurances seem barely, temporarily compatible. Yet risks of rule lie quite as much in bureaucratic momentum as in presidential misjudgment. Frustrated, uncomprehending bureaucrats can be as much a danger to us all, and to a President, as faults in his own knowledge, or his judgment, or his temperament. The check and balance system we encounter in the Missile Age does not appear to check or balance its destructive hazards. Rather, it may readily enlarge them. For this there is no help in sight from any source except the human qualities of prudence, luck, and fortitude displayed in 1962 by fourteen men for thirteen days.

A CONSTITUTIONAL ISSUE?

Our Constitution is a product of the eighteenth century. Its authors were men of the Enlightenment and also men of action: political philosophers—mostly at second-hand—with firsthand practical experience. They were intensely conscious of the *paradox of rulership* as manifested by the course of history up to their time. On the one hand, the common good required that political power be placed in some human hands. Only by yielding considerable discretion to a central public authority could citizens secure the common defense, law, order, or personal liberties. But on the other hand, to establish a powerful public authority was to create enormous risks of the misuse of power. As so often before, the rulers, being human and thus fallible, might choose unwisely, or might implement their choices clumsily, at awful cost. Our Constitution makers aimed at an effective central government, else they would not have come to Philadelphia. But they sought to minimize the risks.

The product of their work had four distinctive features. One of these was limited authority: the federal Bill of Rights and its state counterparts were meant to wall off civil liberties, including private property, from arbitrary governmental action. A second feature was shared powers: federal and state governments had overlapping functions, and within the federal structure, so did President, House, Senate, Supreme Court. A third feature was separated institutions: each power-sharing body had a separate base of political accountability, hence constituency, and these were kept distinct from one another. A fourth feature was legitimation by the symbols of popular sovereignty: the people replaced the monarchy, and this was done in such a way as to clothe institutions with their status, while yielding little to direct democracy.

Throughout, the underlying theme was checks and balances: rights hedging authority, powers checking powers, separate institutions in enforced collaboration, with political accountability divided and legitimacy dispersed. No man was entrusted with unlimited prerogatives; neither was the mob. Instead, a goodly group of men, each with a piece of power, backed by a constituency, would scrutinize each other, balancing each other, as they tried to fit their pieces into governance. Thus human failings might be cancelled out.

Then as now the ultimate expression of authority was war, and there this general pattern was applied with special care. The model evidently was the English royal prerogative as modified by Parliament's control over the purse. Our Constitution-makers modified it further. Congress as a substitute for Parliament would also declare war. The Senate as a parliamentary body was to share in making treaties of alliance or of peace. Our President, as substitute for King, had no prerogative to do these things alone. What he retained, alone, was actual command of such armed forces as Congressional enactments gave him leave to raise and keep. It thus was the intention that recourse to war required a *collaborative* judgment by the whole body of men in national elective office. Presidents could not declare war, congressmen could not deploy the troops. On this as on all lesser issues, these men were to check and balance one another.

Yet from the start of our development under the Constitution, Presidents have sent troops into battle without declarations of war. This has occurred quite regularly since Thomas Jefferson dispatched marines against the Barbary pirates.* Moreover, of the conflicts known to us

---

* If one includes all instances in which American armed forces were used by Executive discretion—military as well as presidential—against the forces and persons of other countries without a declaration of war, the list numbers over one hundred. For a partial listing, see U.S., Department of State, *Right to Protect Citizens in Foreign Countries by Landing Force,* memorandum of the Solicitor for the Department of State, 3rd rev. ed., 1934. Among the more important were Polk's occupation of the Mexican border territory, Wilson's interventions in Mexico and Siberia, and interventions in the Dominican Republic by no fewer than four Presidents.

as "wars," three of the four most costly—measured by both life and money—have been undeclared: the Civil War, the Korean War, and now Vietnam. Had war begun in October 1962, its aftermath, perforce, would also have been undeclared.

The Civil War began, in Northern eyes, as a rebellion. In 1861, when South Carolina seized Fort Sumter, Congress was out of session with its Southerners beyond recall. Korea and Vietnam, however, are another matter: both were foreign wars and both began when Congress was in session. In 1950 and in 1965 the Presidents concerned did not apply to Congress. Instead they used their own command authority to send forces into war without a declaration. So did Nixon when our forces crossed the border of Cambodia. So would Kennedy have done, it seems, had there been a third week of crisis over Cuba.

Thirteen Days affords us many clues as to why modern Presidents have shied away from Congress in making decisions about war. One clue is *secrecy*. Before announcing the first step in his response, Kennedy could not disclose to anyone who lacked a rigid "need to know" what the U-2 had discovered. Had the discovery been widely known within the government, it would have leaked out. Had it leaked, the Administration's diplomatic initiative, achieved by making a countermove when unmasking Soviet duplicity, would have been lost. As it turned out, this was perhaps the best kept secret in American history. But only barely. By Saturday, James Reston of the *New York Times* had the story. A phone call from the President to his editor was necessary to delay the story until after the White House announcement.

A second clue is *flexibility*. It took extraordinary care and subtlety to find the "right" first-step response to Soviet missiles. Equal care was needed to design that step so that it signaled our intention to the Soviets, specified clearly what we wanted of Khrushchev, and left Kennedy poised for the next round. In that process, he could not commit himself to anyone without forfeiting maneuver room in dealing with Khrushchev.

Third, flexibility is compounded by *uncertainty.* Soviet intentions were the riddle to be read. These did not declare themselves with any blinding light like the Japanese attack in 1941. Uncertainty is compounded by *complexity.* To marshall our own forces and deploy them, and control them, to persuade our allies; to inform a hundred other governments through the United Nations; to say enough, but not too much in public; meanwhile trying to communicate effectually with Moscow—all this was to load a staggering burden on men already encumbered by innumerable governmental tasks. Finally, everything is compounded by *time.* Everything had to be done almost at once, under the relentless pressure of contemporary technology. Dispatch was of the essence.

Taken together, these factors—above all, time—limit the number of men with whom the constitutional Commander in Chief can engage in meaningful consultation. To maximize the prospect of a wise and viable choice, some interests cannot be excluded. In the missile crisis the issue was pre-eminently a matter of *defense* and *diplomacy;* it depended throughout on the capability of our *intelligence* and posed the possibility of *military* action. As constituted, the Ex Comm assured representation of these interests. Natural parochialism, stemming from the governmental positions of these men, guaranteed that considerations of defense, diplomacy, intelligence, and military action would be voiced. But, potentially, the life of the nation was at stake. How was this interest represented? By the President himself, with aides of his own choosing, not least RFK.

Time made the presidential mind the only source

available from which to draw politically legitimated judgments on what, broadly speaking, can be termed the political feasibilities of contemplated action vis-à-vis our world antagonists: judgments on where history was tending, what opponents could stand, what friends would take, what officials would enforce, what men in the street would tolerate—judgments on the balance of support, opposition, and indifference, at home and abroad.

Where was Congress? What about those other minds legitimated by election? They were out of play, except to have their leadership informed at the last moment. Earlier consultation offered nothing indispensable. Congress, to be sure, could add legitimacy, but of this the President conceived he had enough. As a nationally elective officer he was, himself, more representative than any single congressman or senator and no less representative than all of them together. Besides, command decisions rested constitutionally with his office, not theirs. So he decided first and told them after.

Precursors of those thirteen days were the four days, June 24–27, 1950, from the time the North Koreans crossed the border until we committed troops then occupying Japan. As Kennedy would do some twelve years later, President Truman called into almost continuous session the officials most concerned, foreshadowing the Ex Comm; with their advice he escalated step by step to match successive revelations of North Korean strength and South Korean weakness, sending in observers while appealing to the United Nations, neutralizing Formosa, committing air power, and last committing nearby ground forces. Like Kennedy, Truman informed the Congressional leadership of his command decisions, which were far more generally applauded at the moment than in Kennedy's case. But Truman consciously forbore to seek Congressional action.

Given the necessity for timely choice, and the surrounding circumstances, Truman thought a declaration of war wholly inappropriate. Congressional action of that sort had last been taken in December 1941 against the Axis Powers. Nine years later it implied, both publicly and internationally, not limited hostilities, but rather total war pursued to enemy surrender. Also it implied no other termination than by peace treaty, with Senate ratification, or by resolution of the two houses of Congress. Truman was endeavoring to limit warfare, not to spread it, and to end it expeditiously. He wanted neither his constituents nor the United Nations, nor our allies, nor Moscow, nor Peking, nor—and not least—the Pentagon to view Korea in the guise of World War II. Troops were nearby in Japan. He had command authority to use them. He had four days to decide on their use. In these terms there could be no role for Congress as a partner in decision.

Truman might have made Congress a ratifier of decision. On the fifth day or the sixth he might have sought a resolution of support. In the prevailing climate there is no doubt that he could have got it. He chose not to do so, lest it blur for his successors the command authority at their disposal. Instead he pointed to the United Nations under Senate-approved treaty, justified his action by a United Nations resolution, and asked Congress for the money and controls to prosecute the war. Congress complied. As the fighting dragged on after Chinese intervention, however, Truman paid a heavy political price for failing to make Congress share his June decision. This became "Truman's war." To it can be attributed the defeat of Truman's party in the 1952 elections and the Presidency of Dwight D. Eisenhower.

Conscious of this cost to Truman, the Eisenhower Administration devised a protective means of *pre*-associating Congress with command decision, the "Quemoy-Matsu" formula, which Speaker of the House Sam Rayburn characterized at the time as a "blank check." This was a Congressional resolution covering a given geographic area, which authorized the President to do no more than he had constitutional authority to do: employ armed force if circumstances should warrant. As pioneered by Eisenhower, this formula required first such tension in the area that patriotic congressmen could not refuse, and second such good fortune that the future use of force, if any, was short-lived. Eisenhower twice employed the formula, meeting both requirements, once off the China coast, once in the Middle East. It remained for Lyndon Johnson to employ it in Vietnam.

Of these requirements, Vietnam met the first but missed the second. A naval incident off North Vietnam sufficed for the Tonkin Gulf Resolution, but the use of force proved not to be short-lived. After Americanization of the Vietnam War in the first seven months of 1965, Johnson could have had Congress ratify his decision. Like Truman, he refused. To do so would have meant public acknowledgment that we had entered upon large-scale hostilities likely to last several years. This would have precluded a low-posture, low-visibility approach; it would have precipitated sharp divisions between "hawks" and "doves," subjecting the war effort to intense pressures from each. Moreover, proclamation of sustained hostilities, accompanied by calls for troops and taxes, almost certainly would have delayed or set aside Congressional action on the legislative program for the "Great Society."

As months of war turned into years, however, the President stood alone, a lightning rod for dissent. Having never committed themselves to an American war in Vietnam, members of the Senate and House felt free to attack "Johnson's war." Formally, the Tonkin Gulf Resolution of 1964 may have covered the President's course. Politically, it was a flimsy shield. In considering it initially, the Senate had rejected an amendment stating that Congress did not endorse "extension of the present conflict"; this followed Senator Fulbright's assurance that such an amendment was needless. At the time, President Johnson was opening his campaign for election—against the Republican candidate Barry Goldwater—with word that "American boys should not do the fighting for Asian boys."

Thereafter, once the war had expanded, Congressional disillusion was fueled by a feeling of having been duped. When senators became President Johnson's critics, they tended to attack him sharply and bitterly. Attacks by congressmen helped to legitimate dissent in the country, encouraging others, especially in universities and the media. Moreover, the character of Congressional criticism gave some credibility to charges that the war was not only senseless and immoral, but also illegal. In the end, Johnson's fate, politically, somewhat resembled Truman's.

What does this reading of the recent past suggest about division of warmaking powers between President and Congress? For a nuclear crisis it is hard to fault the balance struck in 1962, tipped all the way toward the President in an Ex Comm. Secrecy, flexibility, uncertainty, and urgency—each alone makes a strong argument. Representation for essential interests underlines it. Together these impel the view that when a nuclear exchange impends, formal Congressional participation is not only inconvenient, but impracticable. In the missile crisis, if presidential decision had escalated to nuclear war, Congressional ratification would have been a mockery, or moot. Here the President is, and probably remains, the nation's Final Arbiter.

But does this logic carry over into warfare of a limited sort, nonnuclear by definition? If not, how are distinctions to be drawn, and how enforced?

It is easy to see why recent Presidents have kept away from Congress, acting on their own responsibility, at such times as June 1950, or July 1965—or April 1970. Indeed their reasons resemble those affecting President Kennedy in October 1962. Many decisions must be made in secret. Congress is notoriously leaky. Skillful bargaining with the antagonist (or even one's allies) requires flexibility. Congressional enactments are not readily amended on short notice. In limited warfare the geography, the weaponry, the scale, and the intensity are all subject to bargaining, overt or tacit. So is termination. A war declared by Congress cannot formally be ended without further act of Congress. And while Americans are more accustomed now than in Korean days to draw distinctions among "wars," the fear of 1950 that an invocation of formalities associated last with World War II might signal an unlimited intent to citizens at home—or governments abroad—still weighed upon the White House as recently as 1965.

Arguments like these led President Johnson to prosecute the Vietnam War at a substantial price, the price of foregoing "war powers," constitutional and statutory. These confer on the White House vast authority in home-front spheres like economic mobilization, public order, news management. But during the Korean War the Supreme Court decided that these powers flowed only from wars declared by Congress. Rather than see Congress act, Johnson dispensed with the authority. President Nixon follows the same course. This suggests how strong the case appears, at least from the perspective of two Presidents.

Yet Vietnam's cost, both human and material, and its duration, coupled with the absence of agreed success or even agreed purpose, has brought into being an opposed perspective, strongly espoused in the Senate, the more so as White House legitimacy has been subject to sustained attack from a variety of sources in the country. Not since Korea has there been so much discussion of the need, and of assorted means, to limit presidential freedom on the military side of foreign policy. And where President Truman was denounced for failing to employ more force, fight wider war, win "victory," President Nixon's sharpest critics take the opposite tack. So did President Johnson's.

The current counterargument, opposing White House logic, is least of all a matter of form, much more a matter of substance. The issue is not literal adherence to the Constitution's terms but rather functional equivalence for their intent, namely that the body of elected men on Capitol Hill share in White House decisions at the time warfare begins. The power of the purse does not suffice; withholding funds from forces in the field is not a practicable course for most elective politicians. What is wanted is a voice before those forces get committed beyond recall.

A number of devices aimed at "redressing the constitutional balance" have been proposed in Congress. These span a spectrum from requiring formal action to regularizing informal consultation. Specifically, recent proposals include: (1) a requirement of affirmative legislative action by both houses of Congress for any military hostilities extending beyond thirty days; (2) an option of legislative veto by either house of troop commitments overseas; (3) a statutory prohibition of American military action (or supply) in certain countries; (4) a requirement for presidential consultation, in advance of action, with a select group like the relevant committee chairmen and ranking minority members. Other proposals are sure to be forthcoming as the Vietnam War drags on.

From the perspective of the last twenty years, even the least of these proposals places an extraordinary constraint upon the President. But push back another ten years and all seems ordinary. The great divide is World War II. Right up until Pearl Harbor, Franklin Roosevelt was more constrained than any recent President. Witness the tortuous process by which he transferred fifty overage American destroyers to Great Britain after the fall of France.* No current proposal would seem able to do more than make a future President work as hard as he did in that instance.

Whether Presidents should now be so constrained, and if so how, are matters for judgment. The closer one looks at these proposals the more complicated are the issues to be judged. Issues come in at least six clusters. Everyone concerned has these to weigh:

First, what is the prospect for "good" decisions on war, or the avoidance of war, under the distribution of power and rules of the game envisaged by each proposal? Which proposals offer the highest probability for getting the nation into the wars one prefers we enter, and keeping us out of the wars he prefers we avoid? Obviously, Americans differ on this issue, some favoring World War II, Korea, and Vietnam alike, some wishing we had stayed out of all three, and many drawing distinctions among them.

It is well to recall that in 1812, and again in 1898, Congress rather than the President took the lead in forcing war upon the country. Indeed, the Spanish-American War might have been fought five years earlier had not President Cleveland made plain that he would not wage it even if Congress declared it.

Second, however one answers the first question "on the average," what about the next case, say in Southeast Asia or the Middle East? Under each proposed realignment of power, what are the prospects for "appropriate" choice? Again, there is obvious disagreement among Americans on what may be appropriate.

Third, how does each proposal fare as a mechanism for resolving differences among Americans over the de-

* See Warren F. Kimball, *The Most Unsordid Act: Lend-Lease 1939–1941* (Baltimore: Johns Hopkins Press, 1969), pp. 67–71; also Robert E. Sherwood, *Roosevelt and Hopkins* (New York: Harper, 1948), pp. 174–76.

cision to enter war? What are its prospects for producing politically viable decisions about war? Is the process one that most citizens recognize as legitimate for making such important decisions about issues on which the nation may be sharply divided?

Fourth, how will each proposed realignment affect the personal power of particular individuals now on the Washington scene? For those involved in making choices about these proposals, the importance of this consideration is clear. For those of us who watch from a distance, the effect of realignments on the influence of our political champions—and their opponents—is important.

Fifth, what is the likelihood of action on each proposal? At any given time, what seem to be prevailing attitudes in press and public? How strongly are these shared by whom in Congress? Where are they placed on which committees in which house? Who else is to be reached, by whom, and how? Legislation calls for successive majorities starting with subcommittees. Short of a tidal wave of public sentiment, one cannot count on legislative action without counting heads.

Finally, what of unintended side effects? These are the bane of constitutional reforms adopted to keep some contemporary problem from ever occurring again. The Twentieth Amendment is a classic case. In order to avoid, forevermore, the crisis that ensued in the four months from FDR's election to inaugural, we so shortened the learning time for Presidents-elect as to invite fiascos like the Bay of Pigs.

These issues share a common characteristic. None is abstractly "constitutional"; all are concretely political. So are the causes of concern behind them. So will be the results. Politically these issues are alive as products of Vietnam, once "Johnson's war," now Nixon's. Their resolution probably is bound up with its outcome. The connection is a matter partly of specifics, from Cambodian invasions to Laotian incursions to whatever next fuels Congressional opposition. More important for the longer run is memory, not in terms befitting a historian but in the looser terms of popular impression.

Thirty years ago, what constrained Franklin Roosevelt was not alone, or even mainly, words in statutes, but rather the forbidding strength of isolationist convictions moving millions of his fellow citizens. What fueled their convictions? A deeply held impression that American involvement in the First World War had been a needless waste, a plot for profit.

Twenty years ago, or ten, or even five, the freedom, relatively speaking, felt and asserted by successive Presidents reflected not alone Congressional but also widespread press and public sentiment. What fueled this permissiveness? Above all "Munich" as remembered after victory in World War II.

Ten years hence we think the "balance" between President and Congress will be no less affected by the net impression of our longest war.

Documents

ADDRESS BY PRESIDENT KENNEDY
OCTOBER 22, 1962

Good evening, my fellow citizens. This Government, as promised, has maintained the closest surveillance of the Soviet military build-up on the island of Cuba. Within the past week unmistakable evidence has established the fact that a series of offensive missile sites is now in preparation on that imprisoned island. The purposes of these bases can be none other than to provide a nuclear strike capability against the Western Hemisphere.

Upon receiving the first preliminary hard information of this nature last Tuesday morning (October 16) at 9:00 A.M., I directed that our surveillance be stepped up. And having now confirmed and completed our evaluation of the evidence and our decision on a course of action, this Government feels obliged to report this new crisis to you in fullest detail.

The characteristics of these new missile sites indicate two distinct types of installations. Several of them include medium-range ballistic missiles capable of carrying a nuclear warhead for a distance of more than 1,000 nautical miles. Each of these missiles, in short, is capable of striking Washington, D.C., the Panama Canal, Cape Canaveral, Mexico City, or any other city in the southeastern part of the United States, in Central America, or in the Caribbean area.

Additional sites not yet completed appear to be designed for intermediate-range ballistic missiles capable of traveling more than twice as far—and thus capable of striking most of the major cities in the Western Hemisphere, ranging as far north as Hudson Bay, Canada, and as far south as Lima, Peru. In addition, jet bombers, capable of carrying nuclear weapons, are now being uncrated and assembled in Cuba, while the necessary air bases are being prepared.

This urgent transformation of Cuba into an important strategic base—by the presence of these large, long-range, and clearly offensive weapons of sudden mass destruction—constitutes an explicit threat to the peace and security of all the

Americas, in flagrant and deliberate defiance of the Rio Pact of 1947, the traditions of this nation and Hemisphere, the Joint Resolution of the 87th Congress, the Charter of the United Nations, and my own public warnings to the Soviet on September 4 and 13.

This action also contradicts the repeated assurances of Soviet spokesmen, both publicly and privately delivered, that the arms build-up in Cuba would retain its original defensive character and that the Soviet Union had no need or desire to station strategic missiles on the territory of any other nation.

The size of this undertaking makes clear that it has been planned for some months. Yet only last month, after I had made clear the distinction between any introduction of ground-to-ground missiles and the existence of defensive antiaircraft missiles, the Soviet Government publicly stated on September 11 that, and I quote, "The armaments and military equipment sent to Cuba are designed exclusively for defensive purposes," and, and I quote the Soviet Government, "There is no need for the Soviet Government to shift its weapons for a retaliatory blow to any other country, for instance Cuba," and that, and I quote the Government, "The Soviet Union has so powerful rockets to carry these nuclear warheads that there is no need to search for sites for them beyond the boundaries of the Soviet Union." That statement was false.

Only last Thursday, as evidence of this rapid offensive build-up was already in my hand, Soviet Foreign Minister Gromyko told me in my office that he was instructed to make it clear once again, as he said his Government had already done, that Soviet assistance to Cuba, and I quote, "pursued solely the purpose of contributing to the defense capabilities of Cuba," that, and I quote him, "training by Soviet specialists of Cuban nationals in handling defensive armaments was by no means offensive," and that "if it were otherwise," Mr. Gromyko went on, "the Soviet Government would never become involved in rendering such assistance." That statement also was false.

Neither the United States of America nor the world community of nations can tolerate deliberate deception and offensive threats on the part of any nation, large or small. We no longer live in a world where only the actual firing of weapons represents a sufficient challenge to a nation's security to constitute maximum peril. Nuclear weapons are so destructive and ballistic missiles are so swift that any substantially increased possibility of their use or any sudden change in their deployment may well be regarded as a definite threat to peace.

For many years both the Soviet Union and the United States, recognizing this fact, have deployed strategic nuclear weapons with great care, never upsetting the precarious status quo which insured that these weapons would not be used in the absence of some vital challenge. Our own strategic missiles have never been transferred to the territory of any other nation under a cloak of secrecy and deception; and our history, unlike that of the Soviets since the end of World War II, demonstrates that we have no desire to dominate or conquer any other nation or impose our system upon its people. Nevertheless, American citizens have become adjusted to living daily on the bull's eye of Soviet missiles located inside the U.S.S.R. or in submarines.

In that sense missiles in Cuba add to an already clear and present danger—although it should be noted the nations of Latin America have never previously been subjected to a potential nuclear threat.

But this secret, swift, and extraordinary build-up of Communist missiles—in an area well known to have a special and historical relationship to the United States and the nations of the Western Hemisphere, in violation of Soviet assurances, and in defiance of American and hemispheric policy—this sudden, clandestine decision to station strategic weapons for the first time outside of Soviet soil—is a deliberately provocative and unjustified change in the status quo which cannot be accepted by this country if our courage and our commitments are ever to be trusted again by either friend or foe.

The 1930's taught us a clear lesson: Aggressive conduct, if allowed to grow unchecked and unchallenged, ultimately leads to war. This nation is opposed to war. We are also true to our word. Our unswerving objective, therefore, must be to prevent the use of these missiles against this or any other country and to secure their withdrawal or elimination from the Western Hemisphere.

Our policy has been one of patience and restraint, as befits a peaceful and powerful nation, which leads a worldwide alliance. We have been determined not to be diverted from our central concerns by mere irritants and fanatics. But now further action is required—and it is underway; and these actions may only be the beginning. We will not prematurely or unnecessarily risk the costs of worldwide nuclear war in which even the fruits of victory would be ashes in our mouth—but neither will we shrink from that risk at any time it must be faced.

Acting, therefore, in the defense of our own security and of the entire Western Hemisphere, and under the authority entrusted to me by the Constitution as endorsed by the resolution of the Congress, I have directed that the following initial steps be taken immediately:

First: To halt this offensive build-up, a strict quarantine on all offensive military equipment under shipment to Cuba is being initiated. All ships of any kind bound for Cuba from whatever nation or port will, if found to contain cargoes of offensive weapons, be turned back. This quarantine will be extended, if needed, to other types of cargo and carriers. We are not at this time, however, denying the necessities of life as the Soviets attempted to do in their Berlin blockade of 1948.

Second: I have directed the continued and increased close surveillance of Cuba and its military build-up. The Foreign Ministers of the Organization of American States in their communiqué of October 3 rejected secrecy on such matters in this Hemisphere. Should these offensive military preparations continue, thus increasing the threat to the Hemisphere, further action will be justified. I have directed the Armed Forces to prepare for any eventualities; and I trust that in the interests of both the Cuban people and the Soviet technicians at the sites, the hazards to all concerned of continuing this threat will be recognized.

Third: It shall be the policy of this nation to regard any nuclear missile launched from Cuba against any nation in the Western Hemisphere as an attack by the Soviet Union on the United States, requiring a full retaliatory response upon the Soviet Union.

Fourth: As a necessary military precaution I have reinforced our base at Guantanamo, evacuated today the dependents of our personnel there, and ordered additional military units to be on a standby alert basis.

Fifth: We are calling tonight for an immediate meeting of the Organ of Consultation, under the Organization of American States, to consider this threat to hemispheric security and to invoke articles six and eight of the Rio Treaty in support of all necessary action. The United Nations Charter allows for regional security arrangements—and the nations of this Hemisphere decided long ago against the military presence of outside powers. Our other allies around the world have also been alerted.

Sixth: Under the Charter of the United Nations, we are asking tonight that an emergency meeting of the Security Council be convoked without delay to take action against this latest Soviet threat to world peace. Our resolution will call for the prompt dismantling and withdrawal of all offensive weapons in Cuba, under the supervision of United Nations observers, before the quarantine can be lifted.

Seventh and finally: I call upon Chairman Khrushchev to halt and eliminate this clandestine, reckless, and provocative threat to world peace and to stable relations between our two nations. I call upon him further to abandon this course of world domination and to join in an historic effort to end the perilous arms race and transform the history of man. He has an opportunity now to move the world back from the abyss of destruction —by returning to his Government's own words that it had no need to station missiles outside its own territory, and withdrawing these weapons from Cuba—by refraining from any action which will widen or deepen the present crisis—and then by participating in a search for peaceful and permanent solutions.

This nation is prepared to present its case against the Soviet threat to peace, and our own proposals for a peaceful world, at any time and in any forum in the Organization of American States, in the United Nations, or in any other meeting that could be useful—without limiting our freedom of action.

We have in the past made strenuous efforts to limit the spread of nuclear weapons. We have proposed the elimination of all arms and military bases in a fair and effective disarmament treaty. We are prepared to discuss new proposals for the removal of tensions on both sides—including the possibilities of a genuinely independent Cuba, free to determine its own destiny. We have no wish to war with the Soviet Union, for we are a peaceful people who desire to live in peace with all other peoples.

But it is difficult to settle or even discuss these problems in an atmosphere of intimidation. That is why this latest Soviet threat—or any other threat which is made either independently or in response to our actions this week—must and will be met with determination. Any hostile move anywhere in the world against the safety and freedom of peoples to whom we are committed—including in particular the brave people of West Berlin —will be met by whatever action is needed.

Finally, I want to say a few words to the captive people of Cuba, to whom this speech is being directly carried by special radio facilities. I speak to you as a friend, as one who knows of your deep attachment to your fatherland, as one who shares your aspirations for liberty and justice for all. And I have watched and the American people have watched with deep sorrow how your nationalist revolution was betrayed and how your fatherland fell under foreign domination. Now your leaders are no longer Cuban leaders inspired by Cuban ideals. They are puppets and agents of an international conspiracy which has turned Cuba against your friends and neighbors in the Americas—and turned it into the first Latin American country to become a target for nuclear war, the first Latin American country to have these weapons on its soil.

These new weapons are not in your interest. They contribute nothing to your peace and well being. They can only undermine it. But this country has no wish to cause you to suffer or to impose any system upon you. We know that your lives and land are being used as pawns by those who deny you freedom.

Many times in the past Cuban people have risen to throw out tyrants who destroyed their liberty. And I have no doubt that most Cubans today look forward to the time when they will be truly free—free from foreign domination, free to choose their own leaders, free to select their own system, free to own their own land, free to speak and write and worship without fear or degradation. And then shall Cuba be welcomed back to the society of free nations and to the associations of this Hemisphere.

My fellow citizens, let no one doubt that this is a difficult and dangerous effort on which we have set out. No one can foresee precisely what course it will take or what costs or casualties will be incurred. Many months of sacrifice and self-discipline lie ahead—months in which both our patience and our will will be tested, months in which many threats and denunciations will keep us aware of our dangers. But the greatest danger of all would be to do nothing.

The path we have chosen for the present is full of hazards, as all paths are; but it is the one most consistent with our character and courage as a nation and our commitments around the world. The cost of freedom is always high—but Americans have always paid it. And one path we shall never choose, and that is the path of surrender or submission.

Our goal is not the victory of might but the vindication of right—not peace at the expense of freedom, but both peace and freedom, here in this Hemisphere and, we hope, around the world. God willing, that goal will be achieved.

WHITE HOUSE STATEMENT ON CONTINUATION OF MISSILE BUILD-UP IN CUBA
OCTOBER 26, 1962

The development of ballistic missile sites in Cuba continues at a rapid pace. Through the process of continued surveillance directed by the President, additional evidence has been acquired which clearly reflects that as of Thursday, October 25, definite build-ups in these offensive missile sites continued to be made. The activity at these sites apparently is directed at achieving a full operational capability as soon as possible.

There is evidence that as of yesterday, October 25, considerable construction activity was being engaged in at the intermediate-range ballistic missile sites. Bulldozers and cranes were observed as late as Thursday actively clearing new areas within the sites and improving the approach roads to the launch pads.

Since Tuesday, October 23, missile-related activities have continued at the medium-range ballistic missiles sites resulting in progressive refinements at these facilities. For example, missiles were observed parked in the open on October 23. Surveillance on October 25 revealed that some of these same missiles have now been moved from their original parked positions. Cabling can be seen running from the missile-ready tents to power generators nearby.

In summary, there is no evidence to date indicating that there is any intention to dismantle or discontinue work on these missile sites. On the contrary the Soviets are rapidly continuing their construction of missile support and launch facilities, and serious attempts are under way to camouflage their efforts.

SECOND ° LETTER FROM CHAIRMAN KHRUSHCHEV TO PRESIDENT KENNEDY
OCTOBER 26, 1962

Dear Mr. President:

It is with great satisfaction that I studied your reply to Mr. U Thant on the adoption of measures in order to avoid contact by our ships and thus avoid irreparable fatal consequences. This reasonable step on your part persuades me that you are showing solicitude for the preservation of peace, and I note this with satisfaction.

I have already said that the only concern of our people and government and myself personally as chairman of the Coun-

° On Friday, Oct. 26, Khrushchev sent two letters to President Kennedy. The first, not made public, apparently took the "soft" line that Russia would remove its missiles from Cuba in return for ending of the U.S. quarantine and assurances that the U.S. would not invade Cuba. The second took a harder line seeking the removal of U.S. missiles in Turkey in return for taking Russian missiles out of Cuba. [A notation from *Congressional Quarterly*]

cil of Ministers is to develop our country and have it hold a worthy place among all people of the world in economic competition, advance of culture and arts, and the rise in people's living standards. This is the loftiest and most necessary field for competition which will only benefit both the winner and loser, because this benefit is peace and an increase in the facilities by means of which man lives and obtains pleasure.

In your statement, you said that the main aim lies not only in reaching agreement and adopting measures to avert contact of our ships, and, consequently, a deepening of the crisis, which because of this contact can spark off the fire of military conflict after which any talks would be superfluous because other forces and other laws would begin to operate—the laws of war. I agree with you that this is only a first step. The main thing is to normalize and stabilize the situation in the world between states and between people.

I understand your concern for the security of the United States, Mr. President, because this is the first duty of the president. However, these questions are also uppermost in our minds. The same duties rest with me as chairman of the U.S.S.R. Council of Ministers. You have been worried over our assisting Cuba with arms designed to strengthen its defensive potential—precisely defensive potential—because Cuba, no matter what weapons it had, could not compare with you since these are different dimensions, the more so given up-to-date means of extermination.

Our purpose has been and is to help Cuba, and no one can challenge the humanity of our motives aimed at allowing Cuba to live peacefully and develop as its people desire. You want to relieve your country from danger and this is understandable. However, Cuba also wants this. All countries want to relieve themselves from danger. But how can we, the Soviet Union and our government, assess your actions which, in effect, mean that you have surrounded the Soviet Union with military bases, surrounded our allies with military bases, set up military bases literally around our country, and stationed your rocket weapons at them? This is no secret. High-placed American officials demonstratively declare this. Your rockets are stationed in Britain and in Italy and pointed at us. Your rockets are stationed in Turkey.

You are worried over Cuba. You say that it worries you because it lies at a distance of ninety miles across the sea from the shores of the United States. However, Turkey lies next to us. Our sentinels are pacing up and down and watching each other. Do you believe that you have the right to demand security for your country and the removal of such weapons that you qualify as offensive, while not recognizing this right for us?

You have stationed devastating rocket weapons, which you call offensive, in Turkey literally right next to us. How then does recognition of our equal military possibilities tally with such unequal relations between our great states? This does not tally at all.

It is good, Mr. President, that you agreed for our representatives to meet and begin talks, apparently with the participation of U.N. Acting Secretary General U Thant. Consequently, to some extent, he assumes the role of intermediary, and we believe that he can cope with the responsible mission if, of course, every side that is drawn into this conflict shows good will.

I think that one could rapidly eliminate the conflict and normalize the situation. Then people would heave a sigh of relief, considering that the statesmen who bear the responsibility have sober minds, and awareness of their responsibility, and an ability to solve complicated problems and not allow matters to slide to the disaster of war.

This is why I make this proposal: We agree to remove those weapons from Cuba which you regard as offensive weapons. We agree to do this and to state this commitment in the United Nations. Your representatives will make a statement to the effect that the United States, on its part, bearing in mind the anxiety and concern of the Soviet state, will evacuate its analogous weapons from Turkey. Let us reach an understanding on what time you and we need to put this into effect.

After this, representatives of the U.N. Security Council could control on-the-spot the fulfillment of these commitments. Of course, it is necessary that the Governments of Cuba and Turkey would allow these representatives to come to their countries and check fulfillment of this commitment, which each side undertakes. Apparently, it would be better if these representatives enjoyed the trust of the Security Council and ours—the United States and the Soviet Union—as well as of Turkey and

Cuba. I think that it will not be difficult to find such people who enjoy the trust and respect of all interested sides.

We, having assumed this commitment in order to give satisfaction and hope to the peoples of Cuba and Turkey and to increase their confidence in their security, will make a statement in the Security Council to the effect that the Soviet Government gives a solemn pledge to respect the integrity of the frontiers and the sovereignty of Turkey, not to intervene in its domestic affairs, not to invade Turkey, not to make available its territory as a *place d'armes* for such invasion, and also will restrain those who would think of launching an aggression against Turkey either from Soviet territory or from the territory of other states bordering on Turkey.

The U.S. Government will make the same statement in the Security Council with regard to Cuba. It will declare that the United States will respect the integrity of the frontiers of Cuba, its sovereignty, undertakes not to intervene in its domestic affairs, not to invade and not to make its territory available as [a] *place d'armes* for the invasion of Cuba, and also will restrain those who would think of launching an aggression against Cuba either from U.S. territory or from the territory of other states bordering on Cuba.

Of course, for this we would have to reach agreement with you and to arrange for some deadline. Let us agree to give some time, but not to delay, two or three weeks, not more than a month.

The weapons on Cuba, that you have mentioned and which, as you say, alarm you, are in the hands of Soviet officers. Therefore any accidental use of them whatsoever to the detriment of the United States of America is excluded. These means are stationed in Cuba at the request of the Cuban Government and only in defensive aims. Therefore, if there is no invasion of Cuba, or an attack on the Soviet Union, or other of our allies then, of course, these means do not threaten anyone and will not threaten. For they do not pursue offensive aims.

If you accept my proposal, Mr. President, we would send our representatives to New York, to the United Nations, and would give them exhaustive instructions in order to come to terms sooner. If you would also appoint your men and give them appropriate instructions, this problem could be solved soon.

Why would I like to achieve this? Because the entire world is now agitated and expects reasonable actions from us. The greatest pleasure for all the peoples would be an announcement on our agreement, on nipping in the bud the conflict that has arisen. I attach great importance to such understanding because it might be a good beginning and, specifically, facilitate a nuclear test ban agreement. The problem of tests could be solved simultaneously, not linking one with the other, because they are different problems. However, it is important to reach an understanding to both these problems in order to make a good gift to the people, to let them rejoice in the news that a nuclear test ban agreement has also been reached and thus there will be no further contamination of the atmosphere. Your and our positions on this issue are very close.

All this, possibly, would serve as a good impetus to searching for mutually acceptable agreements on other disputed issues, too, on which there is an exchange of opinion between us. These problems have not yet been solved, but they wait for an urgent solution which would clear the international atmosphere. We are ready for this.

These are my proposals, Mr. President.

Respectfully yours,
(s) NIKITA KHRUSHCHEV

PRESIDENT KENNEDY TO CHAIRMAN KHRUSHCHEV
OCTOBER 27, 1962

[Reply to Chairman Khrushchev's first letter of October 26]

I have read your letter of October 26th with great care and welcomed the statement of your desire to seek a prompt solution to the problem. The first thing that needs to be done, however, is for work to cease on offensive missile bases in Cuba and for all weapons systems in Cuba capable of offensive use to be rendered inoperable, under effective United Nations arrangements.

Assuming this is done promptly, I have given my representatives in New York instructions that will permit them to work out this weekend—in cooperation with the Acting Secretary General and your representative—an arrangement for a permanent solution to the Cuban problem along the lines suggested in your letter of October 26th. As I read your letter, the key elements of your proposals—which seem generally acceptable as I understand them—are as follows:

1) You would agree to remove these weapons systems from Cuba under appropriate United Nations observation and supervision; and undertake, with suitable safeguards, to halt the further introduction of such weapons systems into Cuba.

2) We, on our part, would agree—upon the establishment of adequate arrangements through the United Nations to ensure the carrying out and continuation of these commitments—(a) to remove promptly the quarantine measures now in effect and (b) to give assurances against an invasion of Cuba. I am confident that other nations of the Western Hemisphere would be prepared to do likewise.

If you will give your representative similar instructions, there is no reason why we should not be able to complete these arrangements and announce them to the world within a couple of days. The effect of such a settlement on easing world tensions would enable us to work toward a more general arrangement regarding "other armaments," as proposed in your second letter which you made public. I would like to say again that the United States is very much interested in reducing tension and halting the arms race; and if your letter signifies that you are prepared to discuss a detente affecting NATO and the Warsaw Pact, we are quite prepared to consider with our allies any useful proposals.

But the first ingredient, let me emphasize, is the cessation of work on missile sites in Cuba and measures to render such weapons inoperable, under effective international guarantees. The continuation of this threat, or a prolonging of this discussion concerning Cuba by linking these problems to the broader questions of European and world security, would surely lead to an intensified situation on the Cuban crisis and a grave risk to the peace of the world. For this reason I hope we can quickly agree along the lines outlined in this letter and in your letter of October 26th.

(s) JOHN F. KENNEDY

WHITE HOUSE STATEMENT
OCTOBER 27, 1962

Several inconsistent and conflicting proposals have been made by the U.S.S.R. within the last twenty-four hours, including the one just made public in Moscow. The proposal broadcast this morning involves the security of nations outside the Western Hemisphere. But it is the Western Hemisphere countries and they alone that are subject to the threat that has produced the current crisis—the action of the Soviet Government in secretly introducing offensive weapons into Cuba. Work on these offensive weapons is still proceeding at a rapid pace. The first imperative must be to deal with this immediate threat, under which no sensible negotiations can proceed.

It is therefore the position of the United States that, as an urgent preliminary to consideration of any proposals, work on the Cuban bases must stop; offensive weapons must be rendered inoperable; and further shipment of offensive weapons to Cuba must cease—all under effective international verification.

As to proposals concerning the security of nations outside this hemisphere, the United States and its allies have long taken the lead in seeking properly inspected arms limitation, on both sides. These efforts can continue as soon as the present Soviet-created threat is ended.

CHAIRMAN KHRUSHCHEV TO PRESIDENT KENNEDY
OCTOBER 28, 1962

Dear Mr. President:

I have received your message of 27 October. I express my satisfaction and thank you for the sense of proportion you have displayed and for realization of the responsibility which now devolves on you for the preservation of the peace of the world.

I regard with great understanding your concern and the concern of the United States people in connection with the fact that the weapons you describe as offensive are formidable weapons indeed. Both you and we understand what kind of weapons these are.

In order to eliminate as rapidly as possible the conflict which endangers the cause of peace, to give an assurance to all people who crave peace, and to reassure the American people, all of whom, I am certain, also want peace, as do the people of the Soviet Union, the Soviet Government, in addition to earlier instructions on the discontinuation of further work on weapons constructions sites, has given a new order to dismantle the arms which you described as offensive, and to crate and return them to the Soviet Union.

Mr. President, I should like to repeat what I had already written to you in my earlier messages—that the Soviet Government has given economic assistance to the Republic of Cuba, as well as arms, because Cuba and the Cuban people were constantly under the continuous threat of an invasion of Cuba.

A piratic vessel had shelled Havana. They say that this shelling was done by irresponsible Cuban *émigrés*. Perhaps so. However, the question is from where did they shoot. It is a fact that these Cubans have no territory, they are fugitives from their country, and they have no means to conduct military operations.

This means that someone put into their hands these weapons for shelling Havana and for piracy in the Caribbean in Cuban territorial waters. It is impossible in our time not to notice a piratic ship, considering the concentration in the Caribbean of American ships from which everything can be seen and observed.

In these conditions, pirate ships freely roam around and shell Cuba and make piratic attacks on peaceful cargo ships. It is known that they even shelled a British cargo ship. In a word, Cuba was under the continuous threat of aggressive forces, which did not conceal their intention to invade its territory.

The Cuban people want to build their life in their own

interests without external interference. This is their right, and they cannot be blamed for wanting to be masters of their own country and disposing of the fruits of their own labor. The threat of invasion of Cuba and all other schemes for creating tension over China are designed to strike the Cuban people with a sense of insecurity, intimidate them, and prevent them from peacefully building their new life.

Mr. President, I should like to say clearly once more that we could not remain indifferent to this. The Soviet Government decided to render assistance to Cuba with means of defense against aggression—only with means for defense purposes. We have supplied the defense means which you describe as offensive means. We have supplied them to prevent an attack on Cuba —to prevent rash acts.

I regard with respect and trust the statement you made in your message of 27 October 1962 that there would be no attack, no invasion of Cuba, and not only on the part of the United States, but also on the part of other nations of the Western Hemisphere, as you said in your same message. Then the motives which induced us to render assistance of such a kind to Cuba disappear.

It is for this reason that we instructed our officers—these means as I had already informed you earlier are in the hands of the Soviet officers—to take appropriate measures to discontinue construction of the aforementioned facilities, to dismantle them, and to return them to the Soviet Union. As I had informed you in the letter of 27 October, we are prepared to reach agreement to enable U.N. representatives to verify the dismantling of these means. Thus in view of the assurances you have given and our instructions on dismantling, there is every condition for eliminating the present conflict.

I note with satisfaction that you have responded to the desire I expressed with regard to elimination of the aforementioned dangerous situation as well as with regard to providing conditions for a more thoughtful appraisal of the international situation, fraught as it is with great dangers in our age of thermonuclear weapons, rocketry, spaceships, global rockets, and other deadly weapons. All people are interested in insuring peace.

Therefore, vested with trust and great responsibility, we

must not allow the situation to become aggravated and must stamp out the centers where a dangerous situation fraught with grave consequences to the cause of peace has arisen. If we, together with you, and with the assistance of other people of good will, succeed in eliminating this tense atmosphere, we should also make certain that no other dangerous conflicts, which could lead to a world nuclear catastrophe, would arise.

In conclusion, I should like to say something about a detente between NATO and the Warsaw Treaty countries that you have mentioned. We have spoken about this long since and are prepared to continue to exchange views on this question with you and to find a reasonable solution.

We should like to continue the exchange of views on the prohibition of atomic and thermonuclear weapons, general disarmament, and other problems relating to the relaxation of international tension.

Although I trust your statement, Mr. President, there are irresponsible people who would like to invade Cuba now and thus touch off a war. If we do take practical steps and proclaim the dismantling and evacuation of the means in question from Cuba, in so doing we, at the same time, want the Cuban people to be certain that we are with them and are not absolving ourselves of responsibility for rendering assistance to the Cuban people.

We are confident that the people of all countries, like you, Mr. President, will understand me correctly. We are not threatening. We want nothing but peace. Our country is now on the upsurge. Our people are enjoying the fruits of their peaceful labor. They have achieved tremendous successes since the October Revolution, and created the greatest material, spiritual, and cultural values. Our people are enjoying these values; they want to continue developing their achievements and insure their further development on the way of peace and social progress by their persistent labor.

I should like to remind you, Mr. President, that military reconnaissance planes have violated the borders of the Soviet Union. In connection with this there have been conflicts between us and notes exchanged. In 1960 we shot down your U-2 plane, whose reconnaissance flight over the U.S.S.R. wrecked the summit meeting in Paris. At that time, you took a correct position and denounced that criminal act of the former U[nited] S[tates] administration.

But during your term of office as president another violation of our border has occurred, by an American U-2 plane in the Sakhalin area. We wrote you about that violation on 30 August. At that time you replied that that violation had occurred as a result of poor weather, and gave assurances that this would not be repeated. We trusted your assurance, because the weather was indeed poor in that area at that time.

But had not your plane been ordered to fly about our territory, even poor weather could not have brought an American plane into our airspace, hence, the conclusion that this is being done with the knowledge of the Pentagon, which tramples on international norms and violates the borders of other states.

A still more dangerous case occurred on 28 October, when one of your reconnaissance planes intruded over Soviet borders in the Chukotka Peninsula area in the north and flew over our territory. The question is, Mr. President: How should we regard this? What is this, a provocation? One of your planes violates our frontier during this anxious time we are both experiencing, when everything has been put into combat readiness. Is it not a fact than an intruding American plane could be easily taken for a nuclear bomber, which might push us to a fateful step; and all the more so since the U[nited] S[tates] Government and Pentagon long ago declared that you are maintaining a continuous nuclear bomber patrol?

Therefore, you can imagine the responsibility you are assuming; especially now, when we are living through such anxious times.

I should like also to express the following wish; it concerns the Cuban people. You do not have diplomatic relations. But through my officers in Cuba, I have reports that American planes are making flights over Cuba.

We are interested that there should be no war in the world, and that the Cuban people should live in peace. And besides, Mr. President, it is no secret that we have our people on Cuba. Under a treaty with the Cuban Government we have sent there officers, instructors, mostly plain people: specialists, agronomists, zootechnicians, irrigators, land reclamation specialists, plain workers, tractor drivers, and others. We are concerned about them.

I should like you consider, Mr. President, that violation of Cuban airspace by American planes could also lead to dangerous consequences. And if you do not want this to happen, it would be better if no cause is given for a dangerous situation to arise. We must be careful now and refrain from any steps which would not be useful to the defense of the states involved in the conflict, which could only cause irritation and even serve as a provocation for a fateful step. Therefore, we must display sanity, reason, and refrain from such steps.

We value peace perhaps even more than other peoples because we went through a terrible war with Hitler. But our people will not falter in the face of any test. Our people trust their government, and we assure our people and world public opinion that the Soviet Government will not allow itself to be provoked. But if the provocateurs unleash a war, they will not evade responsibility and the grave consequences a war would bring upon them. But we are confident that reason will triumph, that war will not be unleashed, and peace and the security of the peoples will be insured.

In connection with the current negotiations between Acting Secretary General U Thant and representatives of the Soviet Union, the United States, and the Republic of Cuba, the Soviet Government has sent First Deputy Foreign Minister V. V. Kuznetsov to New York to help U Thant in his noble efforts aimed at eliminating the present dangerous situation.

Respectfully yours,
(s) N. KHRUSHCHEV

STATEMENT BY PRESIDENT KENNEDY ON
RECEIPT OF CHAIRMAN KHRUSHCHEV'S LETTER
OCTOBER 28, 1962

I welcome Chairman Khrushchev's statesmanlike decision to stop building bases in Cuba, dismantling offensive weapons and returning them to the Soviet Union under United Nations verification. This is an important and constructive contribution to peace.

We shall be in touch with the Secretary General of the United Nations with respect to reciprocal measures to assure peace in the Caribbean area.

It is my earnest hope that the governments of the world can, with a solution of the Cuban crisis, turn their urgent attention to the compelling necessity for ending the arms race and reducing world tensions. This applies to the military confrontation between the Warsaw Pact and NATO countries as well as to other situations in other parts of the world where tensions lead to the wasteful diversion of resources to weapons of war.

PRESIDENT KENNEDY TO CHAIRMAN KHRUSHCHEV
OCTOBER 28, 1962

Dear Mr. Chairman:

I am replying at once to your broadcast message of October twenty-eight, even though the official text has not yet reached me, because of the great importance I attach to moving forward promptly to the settlement of the Cuban crisis. I think that you and I, with our heavy responsibilities for the maintenance of peace, were aware that developments were approaching a point where events could have become unmanageable. So I welcome this message and consider it an important contribution to peace.

The distinguished efforts of Acting Secretary General U Thant have greatly facilitated both our tasks. I consider my letter to you of October twenty-seventh and your reply of today as firm undertakings on the part of both governments which should be promptly carried out. I hope that the necessary measures can at once be taken through the United Nations, as your message says, so that the United States in turn will be able to remove the quarantine measures now in effect. I have already made arrangements to report all these matters to the Organization of American States, whose members share a deep interest in a genuine peace in the Caribbean area.

You referred in your letter to a violation of your frontier by an American aircraft in the area of the Chukotsk Peninsula. I have learned that this plane, without arms or photographic equipment, was engaged in an air-sampling mission in connection with your nuclear tests. Its course was direct from Eielson Air Force Base in Alaska to the North Pole and return. In turning south, the pilot made a serious navigational error which carried him over Soviet territory. He immediately made an emergency call on open radio for navigational assistance and was guided back to his home base by the most direct route. I regret this incident and will see to it that every precaution is taken to prevent recurrence.

Mr. Chairman, both of our countries have great unfinished tasks and I know that your people as well as those of the United States can ask for nothing better than to pursue them free from the fear of war. Modern science and technology have given us the possibility of making labor fruitful beyond anything that could have been dreamed of a few decades ago.

I agree with you that we must devote urgent attention to the problem of disarmament, as it relates to the whole world and also to critical areas. Perhaps now, as we step back from danger, we can together make real progress in this vital field. I think we should give priority to questions relating to the proliferation of nuclear weapons, on earth and in outer space, and to the great effort for a nuclear test ban. But we should also work hard to see if wider measures of disarmament can be agreed and put into operation at an early date. The United States government will be prepared to discuss these questions urgently, and in a constructive spirit, at Geneva or elsewhere.

(s) JOHN F. KENNEDY

ADDRESS BY PRESIDENT KENNEDY ON CUBA
NOVEMBER 2, 1962

My fellow citizens: I want to take this opportunity to report on the conclusions which this Government has reached on the basis of yesterday's aerial photographs which will be made available tomorrow, as well as other indications, namely, that the Soviet missile bases in Cuba are being dismantled, their missiles and related equipment are being crated, and the fixed installations at these sites are being destroyed.

The United States intends to follow closely the completion of this work through a variety of means, including aerial surveillance, until such time as an equally satisfactory international means of verification is effected.

While the quarantine remains in effect, we are hopeful that adequate procedures can be developed for international inspection of Cuba-bound cargoes. The International Committee of the Red Cross, in our view, would be an appropriate agent in this matter.

The continuation of these measures in air and sea, until the threat to peace posed by these offensive weapons is gone, is in keeping with our pledge to secure their withdrawal or elimination from this hemisphere. It is in keeping with the resolution of the Organization of American States, and it is in keeping with the exchange of letters with Chairman Khrushchev of October 27th and 28th.

Progress is now being made toward the restoration of peace in the Caribbean, and it is our firm hope and purpose that this progress shall go forward. We will continue to keep the American people informed on this vital matter.

PRESIDENT KENNEDY'S STATEMENT ON CUBA
NOVEMBER 20, 1962

I have today been informed by Chairman Khrushchev that all of the IL-28 bombers now in Cuba will be withdrawn in thirty days. He also agrees that these planes can be observed and counted as they leave. Inasmuch as this goes a long way toward reducing the danger which faced this Hemisphere four weeks ago, I have this afternoon instructed the Secretary of Defense to lift our naval quarantine.

In view of this action I want to take this opportunity to bring the American people up to date on the Cuban crisis and to review the progress made thus far in fulfilling the understandings between Soviet Chairman Khrushchev and myself as set forth in our letters of October 27 and 28. Chairman Khrushchev, it will be recalled, agreed to remove from Cuba all weapons systems capable of offensive use, to halt the further introduction of such weapons into Cuba, and to permit appropriate United Nations observation and supervision to insure the carrying out and continuation of these commitments. We on our part agreed that, once these adequate arrangements for verification had been established, we would remove our naval quarantine and give assurances against invasion of Cuba.

The evidence to date indicates that all known offensive missile sites in Cuba have been dismantled. The missiles and their associated equipment have been loaded on Soviet ships. And our inspection at sea of these departing ships has confirmed that the number of missiles reported by the Soviet Union as having been brought into Cuba, which closely corresponded to our own information, has now been removed. In addition the Soviet Government has stated that all nuclear weapons have been withdrawn from Cuba and no offensive weapons will be reintroduced.

Nevertheless, important parts of the understanding of October 27th and 28th remain to be carried out. The Cuban Government has not yet permitted the United Nations to verify whether all offensive weapons have been removed, and no lasting safeguards have yet been established against the future introduction of offensive weapons back into Cuba.

Consequently, if the Western Hemisphere is to continue to be protected against offensive weapons, this Government has no choice but to pursue its own means of checking on military activities in Cuba. The importance of our continued vigilance is underlined by our identification in recent days of a number of Soviet ground combat units in Cuba, although we are informed that these and other Soviet units were associated with the protection of offensive weapons systems and will also be withdrawn in due course.

I repeat, we would like nothing better than adequate international arrangements for the task of inspection and verification in Cuba, and we are prepared to continue our efforts to achieve such arrangements. Until that is done, difficult problems remain. As for our part, if all offensive weapons are removed from Cuba and kept out of the Hemisphere in the future, under adequate verification and safeguards, and if Cuba is not used for the export of aggressive Communist purposes, there will be peace in the Caribbean. And as I said in September, we shall neither initiate nor permit aggression in this Hemisphere.

We will not, of course, abandon the political, economic, and other efforts of this Hemisphere to halt subversion from Cuba nor our purpose and hope that the Cuban people shall some day be truly free. But these policies are very different from any intent to launch a military invasion of the island.

In short, the record of recent weeks shows real progress, and we are hopeful that further progress can be made. The completion of the commitment on both sides and the achievement of a peaceful solution to the Cuban crisis might well open the door to the solution of other outstanding problems.

May I add this final thought. In this week of Thanksgiving there is much for which we can be grateful as we look back to where we stood only four weeks ago—the unity of this Hemisphere, the support of our allies, and the calm determination of the American people. These qualities may be tested many more times in this decade, but we have increased reason to be confident that those qualities will continue to serve the cause of freedom with distinction in the years to come.

A Short Bibliography and Index

A SHORT BIBLIOGRAPHY

In preparing the Afterword we have reviewed all the published material on the Cuban missile crisis. *Thirteen Days* stands alone, both in its authority as a primary source and in the extent to which its author conveys what it felt like to be there. But a number of other accounts offer supplementary perspectives and additional details.

Students interested in pursuing the missile crisis further are advised to start with Theodore Sorensen's account in *Kennedy* (New York: Harper & Row, 1965). It is the most careful and complete version produced by a central participant. Arthur Schlesinger, Jr.'s *A Thousand Days* (Boston: Houghton Mifflin, 1965) contains additional detail by a professional historian who observed some of the events from a position on the White House staff. Roger Hilsman's *To Move a Nation* (Garden City, N.Y.: Doubleday, 1967) includes an account of the missile crisis from the perspective of a second-level actor in the Department of State. Elie Abel's *The Missile Crisis* (New York: J. B. Lippincott, 1966) offers a more comprehensive chronology of the events, based on extensive interviews with most of the participants, especially in the State Department.

For those who wish to go further, additional references include:

Acheson, Dean, "Homage to Plain Dumb Luck," *Esquire,* February, 1969.

Allison, Graham, *Essence of Decision* (Boston: Little, Brown, 1971).

Horelick, Arnold, and Rush, Myron, *Strategic Power and Soviet Foreign Policy* (Chicago: University of Chicago Press, 1965).

Khrushchev Remembers (Boston: Little, Brown, 1970).

Larson, David, ed., *The Cuban Crisis of 1962* (Boston: Houghton Mifflin, 1963).

Pachter, Henry, *Collision Course* (New York: Frederick A. Praeger, 1963).

A Short Bibliography

Tatu, Michel, *Power in the Kremlin* (New York: Viking Press, 1969).

Taylor, Maxwell, *Memoirs* (New York: W. W. Norton, forthcoming).

U.S. Congress, Senate, Committee on Armed Services, Preparedness Subcommittee, *Interim Report on Cuban Military Build-up*, 88th Congress, 1st Session, 1963.

U.S. Congress, House of Representatives, Committee on Appropriations, Subcommittee on Department of Defense Appropriations, *Hearings*, 88th Congress, 1st Session, 1963.

Weintal, Edward, and Bartlett, Charles, *Facing the Brink* (New York: Charles Scribner's Sons, 1967).

Wohlstetter, Albert and Roberta, "Controlling the Risks in Cuba," Adelphi Papers, No. 17, Institute for Strategic Studies, London, 1965.

Students interested in the Korean analogue may wish to read Glenn D. Paige's *The Korean Decision* (New York: Free Press, 1968).

R. E. N. and G. A.

INDEX

Index

Index